HOLYHEAD
to IRELAND

The *Cambria* in dry dock, Holyhead. (J&C McCutcheon Collection)

HOLYHEAD
to IRELAND

Stena and its Welsh Heritage

JUSTIN P. MERRIGAN *&* IAN H. COLLARD

AMBERLEY

To those who have served with the ships between Holyhead and Ireland over the years; for their service and part in the development of this vital link.

First published 2010

Amberley Publishing Plc
Cirencester Road, Chalford,
Stroud, Gloucestershire, GL6 8PE

www.amberley-books.com

Copyright © Justin P. Merrigan & Ian H. Collard 2010

The right of Justin P. Merrigan & Ian H. Collard to be identified as the Authors
of this work has been asserted in accordance with the
Copyrights, Designs and Patents Act 1988.

British Library Cataloguing in Publication Data.
A catalogue record for this book is available from the British Library.

ISBN 978 1 84868 958 9

Typeset in 10pt on 12pt Sabon.
Typesetting and Origination by Amberley Publishing.
Printed in the UK.

CONTENTS

The historic moment in July 1965 when a car ferry entered Dun Laoghaire for the first time. The *Normannia* lines up for the East Pier ramp with Dover's Captain J. Giddy and Holyhead's Captain Alex Robertson on the bridge of the relief ship. (Justin Merrigan Collection)

An official LNWR postcard issued *c.* 1905. (J&C McCutcheon Collection)

FOREWORD

It gives me much pleasure in writing the Foreword to Justin and Ian's new book as it is so important that the history of trade between Holyhead and Dublin/Dun Laoghaire is preserved, as trade between these two countries means so much to their economic well-being.

I have known Justin since he was a small boy who used to come aboard in Dun Laoghaire with a book, showing drawings and pictures of the Holyhead ships, which were so good that we gave him the run of the ship whilst in port. Even in those days he probably knew more of the history of the passenger ships than the Captain!

The stretch of water between Holyhead and Ireland can vary between a flat calm and some of the most vicious seas imaginable, as I'm sure some of the book's readers will acknowledge! So we can only wonder what the passage was like on some of those early Elizabethan vessels, as there was a fair amount of trade between Holyhead and Ireland even in those days.

I first came into contact with Holyhead just over fifty years ago in 1958. In those days there were three passenger ships sailing between the port and Dun Laoghaire, previously known as Kingstown, and four cattle ships sailing to North Wall in Dublin.

My first ship was the *Slieve Bloom* which I joined as Junior 2nd Officer in April 1958. I had previously sailed with Shaw Savill & Albion Company for nearly ten years trading with Australia and New Zealand. This was quite a shock after Shaw Savill's beautiful passenger ships to find myself on a 1,500 ton cattle vessel! However it was a life I never regretted, as life was both fun and interesting. The Captain and the three Deck Officers all held Foreign-going Masters Certificates, the situation being the same on all the other British Rail vessels.

The two main passenger ships then were the *Cambria* and the *Hibernia*. One would be in Holyhead all day, whilst the other was in Dun Laoghaire. Passengers would join the ship in Holyhead at 9.00 p.m. and were able to go for a drink and a meal, go to bed and find themselves in Dun Laoghaire at 6.45 a.m. the next morning and able to stay on board until 8.00 a.m.

Incidentally, passengers would arrive in Holyhead on the train called the 'Irish Mail'. This was the first train in the world to be given a name.

From Dun Laoghaire the ship sailed at 8.45 p.m. arriving in Holyhead at midnight.

During the summer, the *Cambria* and the *Hibernia* doubled the frequency of their sailings by having an afternoon sailing from Holyhead and a morning sailing from Dun Laoghaire.

The third ship was the much-loved or equally hated *Princess Maud*. She often used to have a daytime sailing or was on standby in case the other two ships were full. But boy, could she roll! Some people would telephone Holyhead to see whether their passage would be aboard her or not, then cancel if it was!

Sailings continued in this fashion until two boys, looking for birds' eggs, accidentally set fire to the Britannia Bridge joining Anglesey with the mainland in May 1970. On watch as Chief Officer on the *Cambria* I could see the red glow in the sky twenty miles away.

The two ships then sailed between Heysham and Holyhead until the new bridge was completed. Thankfully Thomas Telford's suspension bridge was not harmed so that cargo could be brought by road for the cargo ships.

In 1977, by far the best passenger ship to serve the route was built in Aalborg. She was the *St Columba*, a ro-ro vessel fitted with all the latest equipment for her time. Her public rooms and bars were beautifully laid out and she was extremely popular with vehicle drivers and foot passengers. Being able to load and discharge vehicles from either end of the ship resulted in very fast turn-rounds.

I was fortunate to serve on her right from the beginning as Chief Officer. Slowly climbing the ladder I eventually was appointed Senior Captain on her and I retired in 1991 after thirty-three wonderful years in Holyhead.

You will find that this book is full of interesting facts about the history of our business and ships between the two ports. Nobody is such an expert on this than Justin.

I am sure that in these pages you will see how vitally important trade between Holyhead and Dublin/Dun Laoghaire brought so many benefits to our countries. And all this trade was carried out over the centuries. Let us hope that this goes on for many more centuries.

Captain John Bakewell

INTRODUCTION

The Port of Holyhead is operated by Stena Line Ports Ltd, the statutory Harbour Authority. The company took over ownership of the port in 1990 from Sea Containers, who only six years previously assumed control of the harbour as part of the Sealink operation privatised by the Conservative government of the day.

Ranked as the United Kingdom's third-busiest ferry port, after Dover and Portsmouth, Holyhead handled an impressive 1.9 million passengers in 2009. The operation is an impressive one, with world-class tonnage operating for both Stena Line and Irish Ferries on sailings to Dublin Bay. In addition, cruise ship traffic continues to develop and grow, and with the recent availability of the Anglesey Aluminium jetty to the largest cruise ships, the future looks bright for this new trade.

In this book, the authors aim to place on record the heritage on which today's successful port and trade is built – the era of railway ownership, for it is without doubt that Holyhead and the Stena Line routes to Ireland of today owe their existence to the railway companies of yesteryear.

And why should the railways find themselves operating ships? Simply, they saw the benefits of extending their operations beyond the buffers! Co-ordinating rail and sea traffic for passengers, mail and cargo, they built first-rate ships and developed state-of-the-art port facilities, pushing aside irregular and unreliable services which had been run in a rather less than perfect fashion.

The authors' original intention was to cover, in detail, the origins of both Stena Line and Irish Ferries operations at the port, but as the project progressed it became obvious that the history of the latter, back to the days of the City of Dublin Steam Packet, would have to wait for another day. However, it would be impossible to tell the story without reference to this vital contributor in Holyhead's history and so we have included the key aspects of their involvement at the port.

Ian Collard's first visit to Holyhead was to travel on the then-new car ferry *Holyhead Ferry I* to Dun Laoghaire. He caught the 6.05 a.m. train from Rock Ferry to Chester, which connected to the main line service to Holyhead. On arrival, the timings allowed him to walk around the harbour enabling him to photograph the shipping scene of the mid-1960s. The ship itself was impressive, as she was the route's first dedicated car-ferry and was operating sailings in conjunction with the classic mailboats *Cambria* and *Hibernia*. On arrival at the new East Pier berth at Dun Laoghaire, Ian was able to stroll around the harbour to get a closer look at the *Hibernia*, which was resting at her berth. The *Holyhead Ferry 1* was soon unloaded and the speed and efficiency of the operation was evident when he realised she was ready to leave and watched as she quietly slipped away from the car ferry berth.

Ian sailed from Holyhead on the *Cambria* and the *Hibernia* on several occasions after that trip but one of the most unusual day trips was one which offered an afternoon cruise on one of the mailboats from Holyhead to Llandudno Bay. The ship took us down the Anglesey coast, past Puffin Island, the Great Orme and into Llandudno Bay. Unfortunately, the ships were too large to berth at the pier but were able to swing in the bay and then return along the coast to Holyhead.

For Justin Merrigan, Dun Laoghaire Harbour has always been a source of fascination. From the age of five when from the back of his father's car he loved nothing more than to see one of the mailboats at rest on the east side of the Carlisle Pier, through the years until the day he brought his own children to the harbour to view the operations of high-speed craft, the harbour has held a special place in his heart. During his school years, Dun Laoghaire Harbour was his playground. Friendly Harbour Constables and Sealink staff nurtured within him a deep interest in the port's link with Holyhead, served by countless British Rail, Sealink and later Stena Line ferries. How privileged he was to be permitted to view the ferry operations at such close quarters!

He was first introduced to his favourite vantage point, the end of the Carlisle Pier, in 1980 at the age of ten. From there, he was permitted to view the departure of the route's penultimate steam turbine ferry, the *Avalon*. He was hooked! Through the years and the various ships, Justin made lasting friendships with the many Holyhead-based captains, officers and crew members who maintained the crossing day in day out on a year-round basis.

How he loved to stand on the end of the Carlisle Pier during the late 1980s and early 1990s, now with a basic understanding of the art form that is ship handling, and watch as the Master brought his command gently into the berth. Of course, during the winter months it could be very different! With an easterly gale and low water, the Master's every skill was tested as he brought the *St Columba* alongside, fighting the wind and keeping in mind propeller cavitation with reduced water under his keel.

Now living in Hobart, in the Australian island state of Tasmania, Justin looks back with fondness on his days in and around both Dun Laoghaire and Holyhead harbours. Without hesitation, he can safely say the ships, and the people involved in their operation, shaped his life. Perhaps if the Incat-built *Stena Sea Lynx* had been deployed to any other Stena Line route in 1993 then he might not be living in the Antipodes!

The introduction of the fast craft on the Holyhead–Dun Laoghaire route enabled the operator to offer long day excursions which allowed the passenger to venture further on arrival at the ships destination. The *Stena Sea Lynx* sailed from Holyhead as early as 7.00 a.m. at the weekend, enabling passengers to spend some time in Ireland.

Ian recalls the opportunities offered by the 'Lynx', being able to catch the DART train into Dublin and perhaps spend the day travelling to Belfast or even enjoy the delights of Galway. On return to Dun Laoghaire, he would board the *Stena Hibernia* for the evening passage back to Holyhead.

Today, the new road across Anglesey has improved the journey no end, enabling people to visit Holyhead, view the port and the ships in the harbour or sail to Ireland. The success of the shipping operations in 2010 is evident by the amount of traffic and trade passing through the port and the consequent increase in the size of the vessels on the Holyhead to Dun Laoghaire and Dublin routes.

Justin Merrigan, Hobart, Tasmania
Ian Collard, New Brighton
November 2010

The *Cambria* leaves Dun Laoghaire in the teeth of a westerly gale. (Charles Brinsley Sheridan)

The launch of the *Cambria* at Belfast, 1948. (J&C McCutcheon Collection)

I

Early Beginnings

Holyhead is the main town of Anglesey, an island situated off the north-west coast of Wales. Anglesey, or Ynys Môn in Welsh, is linked with the mainland by road across the Menai Bridge and by rail and road across the Britannia Bridge spanning the Menai Strait. Holyhead itself, however, is actually located on Holy Island, which is linked to Anglesey by the Stanley Embankment, a causeway known locally as the Cob. It was built by Thomas Telford when he constructed the A5 across Anglesey between 1815 and 1823. It was named after W. O. Stanley (1802–84).

The name Anglesey comes from the Norse word 'ongull', which means strait and was described as 'isle of straits'. Around 500 BC, Celtic tribes arrived on the island and the druids brought with them their religion and beliefs. In AD 61, the Roman General Gaius Suetonius Paulinus invaded Anglesey and attempted to break the power of the druids by destroying their shrines and sacred graves. The domination of this part of Roman Britain was directed from a large legionary fortress at Chester and another in the south at the town now known as Caerleon. However, it was the Roman Governor of Britain, Gnaeus Julius Agricola, who brought Anglesey into the Roman Empire in AD 78.

The Romans, who carried on considerable trade with Ireland, built a small fortlet to defend the coast against Irish raiders. The Roman occupation of Britain lasted until the end of the fourth century when they withdrew, leaving Anglesey at the mercy of continued raids. The Irish Picts settled on the island until their defeat by Caswallon Law Hir ap Einion at the battle of Cerrig y Gwyddyl around AD 470. It is claimed that their leader, Sirigi, who was slain by Caswallon, was buried on the south side of the old fort near the church vestry.

In the sixth century, the fort was given to Cybi, a Cornish Bishop, the son of Solomon, Duke of Cornwall. Cybi founded a monastery within the three walls of the fort – the fourth wall being the sea – and it is from him that Holyhead takes its Welsh name of Caergybi, meaning the fortified place, or city of Cybi.

The island was raided by the Danish in AD 853, by Iron Knee and by Sitric the Silken Beard in AD 961 and yet again in AD 987. After the Irish, the island was invaded by Vikings, Saxons, and Normans before falling to Edward I of England in the thirteenth century.

Records indicate that the earliest parts of the church of St Cybi were built in the thirteenth century, together with a monastery and small township. In 1283, King

Edward I visited 'Castrum Cuby' and, by 1315, the town was known as Haliheved, Holiheved in 1332 and Caergybi in 1352. By 1394, it was Le Holyhede and Insulae de St Ceby in the late fifteenth century. A map of Wales shows it as Holy Head or Caer Cybi in 1573 and, in 1783, *Topographica Britannica* states, 'Holyhead, so called from the mountain at the back of it'.

The Romans had established a road through Denbigh and Conway towards the Menai Straits but there was no evidence that this had been continued through Anglesey. It is thought that, through to the reign of Henry VIII, mail to Ireland was probably conveyed by land to Chester and then onwards by sea. When Henry VIII dissolved the monasteries and the Collegiate Establishment of Holyhead, St Cybi's became an ordinary parish church. The following century, the revenues from the church became part of the estate of Dr Gwynne, who bequeathed them to Jesus College at Oxford, which lasted until 1921 when the Church of Wales was disestablished.

In Elizabethan times, the Queen communicated with her Lord Lieutenant in Ireland through Chester and then to Liverpool and between 1573 and 1576 ordinary posts were established through Holyhead. Records of 1578 show that Holy Island was joined to Anglesey by a bridge. Milestones from Holyhead were placed at the side of the road in 1752 and the fourth stone from Holyhead was placed on the bridge. A ford had been established at that point at an early date and there is evidence that the ford was still in use, even after the bridge had been completed.

In June and July 1597, Sir Henry Wallop, Vice-Treasurer for War, experienced difficulties on his journey to Dublin. He sailed from Chester on 22 June but when his vessel reached Ormshead it was driven back to Chester by a storm. He then proceeded to Holyhead by land and hired a flyboat to take him to Dublin. He left Holyhead on 2 July but had to return owing to a change of wind and was still weatherbound at Holyhead until 5 July. In 1599, the journey from London could be accomplished within a fortnight.

When James I was crowned in 1601, he took responsibility for improving the postal system and ensuring that payments for the service were increased to two pence halfpenny per mile and the weight carried by each horse was reduced from 50 lb to 30 lb.

In 1605, a civil servant by the name of John Bingley embarked on a journey between Chester and Ireland. On the fourth attempt, when nearly a quarter of the way across, his ship split her sails and was in danger of foundering in a westerly storm. The pump having broken this put the ship in grave peril but four seamen kept bailing and they eventually got to Beaumaris from where Bingley then made his way to Holyhead. On arrival there, he discovered over 400 people had been waiting at Chester to complete the journey to Ireland and some had been there for seventeen or eighteen weeks. However, most travellers preferred the longer sea crossing than the uncomfortable journey by road across North Wales.

In 1608, a Robert Pepper was Master of the post barque at Holyhead, the vessel nominated by the Master of Posts. Complaints were made about the unsuitability of the vessel, which were refuted by Sir Arthur Chichester, the Lord Deputy. However, in 1625, the post system was improved and the daily pay of some postmasters was increased from 20d to 2s. A post was established at Llangefni around that time, and the amount paid for the hire of a vessel between Holyhead and Dublin was increased to £10 a month. The Treasury minutes described the vessel as 'a boat with furniture to transport the packets to Ireland', which was later changed to 'packet boat'.

The postal service suffered setbacks in the following years until new proposals for the letter post were approved following the accession of Charles I. In 1635, people were able to send letters from London to Dublin for *6d* per letter. However, most travellers still preferred to travel to Ireland from Chester or Parkgate on the River Dee.

On 16 March 1646, the House of Commons resolved that two packet boats should be selected and prepared for a service between Holyhead and Dublin. The following October, the House appointed Captain Stephen Rich, commander of these boats, and the Commissioners of the Navy made a contract with him as from 1 November that year, each boat being paid at the rate of eleven pounds a month.

Shortly before the death of Cromwell in 1658, Major Thomas Swift, the Governor of Holyhead, reported that the coasts were infected with pirates who had taken twelve or thirteen ships belonging to Chester and Liverpool and the Irish mail had been broken open. He was responsible for raising the height of the West Tower of St Cybi's church by 17 feet so that a lookout could have an uninterrupted view out to sea. As well as being Postmaster and Churchwarden Swift was also Commissioner under the Act for the Propagation of the Gospel in Wales between 1650 and 1653. He was able to purchase land around Swift Square and Welch's House was built to accommodate travellers through the port.

Following the restoration of the Monarchy, Sir John Carter replaced Major Thomas Swift and an Act of Parliament was passed which established the Post Office. A John Swift was appointed as contractor for the packet boats between Holyhead and Dublin on a salary of £400 a year for three vessels and a provisional arrangement for a fourth ship on the route. Although the road between Chester and Holyhead was improved in the 1660s, Chester, Parkgate and Neston continued to be used by passengers sailing to Ireland. A Holyhead packet was lost in 1670 with the loss of 120 lives. With two others sinking in the following years, permission was obtained to build a new vessel which would be more suitable for conditions in the Irish Sea.

James Vickers maintained the three packet vessels in 1689 for the amount of £450 a year. The *Grace* was taken over by French privateers on 25 July 1692 while at anchor in Dublin Bay and was stripped and plundered. A ransom of fifty guineas was paid for the return of her hull and Vickers was paid £150 in compensation by the Postmaster who also raised the annual subsidy to £500, an amount that remained at basically the same for the next 100 years as steamers superseded the sailing ships on the route.

Turnpike Trusts, bodies set up by Act of Parliament with powers to collect road tolls for maintaining the principal highways in Britain, were introduced at the beginning of the eighteenth century and the General Post Office in London and the General Letter Office in Dublin were established by Act of Parliament in 1711. It cost sixpence for a letter to be sent from London to Dublin. In 1717, the owner of the island of Skerries, William Trench, was given permission to establish a light for which he was allowed to collect tolls from passing vessels. The light was originally a coal fire, being replaced by oil light in 1804 when the lighthouse was built.

The Irish trade was the main cargo passing through Holyhead at this time, although American sugar and other goods were also discharged at the creek. A customs officer was appointed in 1680 and Hugh Lloyd, who was the salt officer, was appointed as Deputy to the Collector at Beaumaris in 1716. Lewis Morris was responsible for completing a coastal survey of Wales from 1737 to 1742 which was published as *Plans of harbours, bays and roads in St Georges and the Bristol Channel*. He suggested improvements to the harbour at Holyhead, including a pier from Salt Island and the walling up of the sounds between Salt Island and the shore and Parry's Island and Turkey Shore in an attempt to keep the north-east and north-west swell out of the harbour. His brother, William, was Collector of Customs at Holyhead between 1737 and 1763 and described himself as 'Deputy customer, collector, deputy comptroller, comptroller of the coal duties, deputy searcher, coast waiter and searcher, water bailiff, deputy vice-admiral, collector of the Skerry lights, surgeon, florist and botanist to the Garrison of Holyhead'.

By the middle of the eighteenth century, the operator of the three packets was John Power, who received £900 per year and provided vessels slightly larger than their predecessors. By 1763, Thomas Blair received £1,050 to operate the sailing packets *Earl of Bessborough*, the *Hampden* and the *Prendergast*. Five years later, two of these vessels were replaced by the *Lord Treven* and *Fortesque*. Meanwhile, a pier was built at Dunleary in 1765 as an alternative to Dublin's Pigeon House Quay in time of bad weather.

A report by the President Surveyor of the Post Office in 1767 recommended the establishment of three additional packet boats between Dublin and Holyhead, and three additional posts between Dublin and Cork and Dublin and Belfast. In 1768, the three additional vessels entered service providing daily sailings for six days a week between Holyhead and Dublin. However, the number of vessels was reduced to five in 1772 following efficiency savings and the Postmaster General working with several contractors instead of one with agreement to pay a fee of £350 for each vessel employed.

The first vessels used under the new agreement were the *Dartmouth*, *Le Du Spencer*, *Hillsborough*, *Clermont* and the *Bessborough*. The *Bessborough* and the *Hillsborough* were captured by the American privateer *Black Prince* on 8 March 1780. The Post Office paid £453 9s 0d and expenses for the ransom for one vessel and £614 and expenses for the other. Crew were paid 30s a month and £2 maintenance, which came from the contract and the carriage of passengers, goods and carriages.

The stagecoaches started a regular service from Chester to Holyhead in 1785 and improvements in the service meant that the mails arrived in Dublin on the third day rather the fifth. Coaches from London connected to those from Chester and took passengers to the Eagle & Child at Holyhead. This hostelry was built in 1770 and was the main hotel in the town until the Station Hotel was opened nearly one hundred years later.

The timetable was as follows: Depart London at 8 p.m. travelling overnight and arriving at Northampton at 5.25 a.m. After half an hour for breakfast, depart Northampton arriving in Lichfield at 2 p.m. where there was 45 minutes allowed for lunch. After a short break the coach would proceed to Stafford at 5 p.m. where 15 minutes was allowed for tea. Arrive at Chester at midnight where passengers were allowed an hour for supper before proceeding to St Asaph where they arrived at 6 a.m. and stayed for 20 minutes for breakfast. The coach was allowed three hours and twenty-five minutes to reach the River Conway and 30 minutes for the ferry crossing, arriving at Bangor Ferry at 12.40 for lunch at the George & Dragon. It was scheduled to arrive at the Eagle & Child at Holyhead at 5.13 p.m. The Royal Mail coach cost £6 6s od for an inside seat and £3 for the outside. The Ancient Briton coach was priced as £4 4s od inside and £2 10s od inside. The standard, quality and regularity of the service increased its popularity to the public and other services through Parkgate began to decline.

Passengers and mail were embarked and disembarked at Holyhead and Dublin by small wherries. The creek at Holyhead known as the old harbour dried every ebb tide and the sailing packets anchored off Parry's Island. In Dublin, they anchored at the packet moorings near Ringsend. In 1791, it was decided to form a basin, or harbour at the blockhouse, which the Corporation of Dublin had built on the South Wall. When completed, the dock was known as Pigeon-house Dock and cutter sailing packets were able to dock there in shelter.

In 1796, the Chief Secretary of Ireland requested that the Postmaster General of Ireland charter two small vessels which were to be used when the weather conditions were too inclement and rough for the packet boats to sail. Postage charges were increased from 6d to 8d that year. The crossing on the vessels took around twenty hours on average. The wherries each carried a master and six seamen, and the contract rate was £49 2s 6d a month for each vessel. A third wherry was added on 8 June 1793.

The log of the *Bessborough* from 1 March – 26 April 1797 showed that the vessel made nine voyages or eighteen passages, the longest was fifty-two hours, the four shortest were nine, ten, twelve and sixteen hours. All other passages exceeded twenty-one hours, and the average was twelve hours twenty minutes.

Holyhead church.

Holyhead market
place, 1769.

Holyhead Harbour,
1830.

2

Building a Port

As we have seen, Holyhead's place in the communications link between London and Ireland can be traced back to the days of Elizabeth I. Despite its newfound importance, development was, however, painfully slow. Mail packet boats moored alongside Salt Island and passengers and mail were carried to and from the shore in wherries. On the north side of the harbour was the custom house, and a related quay was constructed by building a wall from the shore to a small island in the estuary. A lighthouse was built on the east end of Salt Island, as shown on a print of 1815, though no records exist concerning its construction or operation. Salt Island took its name from the salt works constructed on it, and Lewis Morris's detailed map of 1746 shows this as 'in ruins'.

By the beginning of the nineteenth century, Holyhead was in regular use as a packet station. It was typical of its time in being basic to say the least. At this time, Britain was at war with France and had also suffered rebellion in Ireland. Though not seen as a long-term political solution to the problems in Ireland, an Act of Union was signed on 1 January 1801, which effectively abolished the Irish Parliament and led to 100 Irish members attending at Westminster. This, at least, meant that invasion of Britain from Ireland by the French could now be effectively monitored and dealt with should occasion arise. It also, however, led to considerable pressure being placed upon the Government to improve the route between London and Dublin for the sake of both comfort and speed, and to allow more effective passage for the military.

The Government commissioned John Rennie and Joseph Huddard to survey the route between London and Holyhead in 1801. Their report contained suggestions for improving the road, bridging the Menai Strait and improving the harbours at Holyhead and Howth in Ireland. No immediate work was started, and Thomas Telford was appointed to examine the road again in 1810, after which, in 1815, he was asked to undertake the necessary improvements, including long lengths of new road through Wales, and particularly across Anglesey. The improvements incorporated the building of the Menai Bridge, the new road across Anglesey and the Stanley Embankment across the strait between Anglesey and Holy Island. The Menai Bridge was opened on 30 January 1826, the first iron suspension bridge of its kind in the world. To enable clear passage for ships passing under, the bridge was designed to allow 100 feet of clearance from the span to the water. The pillars were built with stone from Penmon quarry and supported by sixteen chains. To raise the central section of the chain, weighing 23 tons, it took 150 men using block and tackle.

In the meantime, Rennie had been commissioned to undertake improvements at Holyhead Harbour. In 1809, he was asked to draw up plans, and works commenced the following year. His initial plan involved the construction of a pier extending from the small island of Ynys Halen, or Salt Island, with a new road and bridge across to Salt Island. His initial estimate for this work was £66,862, which included the purchase of Salt Island. The Admiralty Pier was largely constructed by 1817, when it was proposed to extend it by a further 120 feet, to be completed by the end of 1818, though works were still ongoing in 1819. The south side of the pier was faced with a perpendicular wall of cut stone while near the east end shelter against east winds and swell was provided by a spur projecting 60 feet at right angles with the wall. The back of the pier was inclined from the top of the parapet, and built with large rough stones.

In 1819, Rennie stated that plans were in hand to construct a graving dock, but that the work was being held up whilst decisions were being made concerning the location of the custom house. In 1821, he wrote to the Admiralty saying that he had drawn up plans for the dry dock to be situated on the south shore of the creek, and for a second pier which would protect the dock and allow greater anchorage space during poor weather when the harbour was used for refuge.

Rennie, who was by now also involved in the construction of the new Asylum Harbour in Dublin Bay at Dunleary, died on 16 October 1821, not of suicide off the unfinished pier at Dunleary as many claim, but of inflammation in the liver, which had afflicted him for some years. By his wife, whom he married in 1789, he left six children, of whom the eldest, George Rennie, followed the same profession as his father. John Rennie was buried with funeral honours in St Paul's Cathedral, near the grave of Sir Christopher Wren.

Thomas Telford was asked to take over responsibility for the harbour works after Rennie's death. His first report to the Commissioners in 1824 stated that great progress had been made in the construction of the new graving dock, and a new road had been made along the side of the harbour, linked to his London to Holyhead Road. Over the next few years the work to the graving dock was completed; a small steam engine was installed in 1828 and the surrounding wall constructed with carpenters shops also provided. On Salt Island, a new custom house and Harbour Master's office were built to a design by Telford. Stores, workers' cottages and workshops were built behind the new offices. Gas lights were installed on the road from the two inns at the west side of the creek to the pier on Salt Island and with all these works the harbour was considered to be 'brought to as perfect a state as was formerly contemplated, [and] it continues not only to afford protection and accommodation to the steam packets, but in stormy weather frequently protects above a hundred sail or coasting vessels'.

In August 1818, the Irish terminal moved from Dublin's Pigeon House to a new harbour at Howth, north of Dublin Bay. From 1 August 1817 to 1 February 1818, the average passage from Holyhead to Dublin was nineteen hours and forty-two minutes; from Dublin to Holyhead was fifteen hours and forty-three minutes. From 1 August 1818 to 1 February 1819, the average from Holyhead to Howth was fourteen hours and fifty-seven minutes, from Howth to Holyhead, fourteen hours and forty-one minutes. But Howth too had its own problems, quickly gaining a poor reputation for its difficult access in easterly gales. With ongoing construction work on the Asylum Harbour at Dunleary, some of the new mail steamers began to use the new berth on the East Pier there in 1827.

In 1819, the Steam Packet Company informed the Postmaster General that they were to establish a packet station at Holyhead and the new steamers *Ivanhoe* and *Talbot* were introduced the following year, cutting the Howth crossing to around eight hours. The mails were, however, still carried in sailing packets and, though the new company offered to contract to take the mails in their steam ships, the Post Office, partly on advice from its captains, continued to use the sailing packets. However, the greater reliability and versatility of the steam ships soon became apparent, and the Post Office, after a trial run, decided to order two steamers. The *Lightning* and the *Meteor* entered service in June 1821.

On 7 August 1821, George IV landed at Holyhead on his way to Ireland, arriving on the yacht *Royal George* escorted by a squadron and spending five days in Anglesey, detained by windy weather. The local newspaper reported that 'His Majesty was struck with admiration at the appearance of the town'. However, the King did not stop at Holyhead and was taken to Plas Newydd for the night by the Marquess of Anglesey to await news of Queen Caroline's health, as it was thought unwise to proceed to Ireland without awaiting events. Having heard that she was improving, he returned to sail the following day, but the winds prevented this. On the following day, he was informed of the death of his estranged Queen, which was marked by the lowering of the masts of the squadron. With weather still hampering his departure to Ireland, it was not until 13 August that he decided to take the steam packet across to Ireland, leaving the squadron at Holyhead to follow when they could. He travelled on the *Lightning*, commanded by Captain John Skinner, and spent the passage eating and drinking until arriving in Howth in quite a state. Departing Ireland through the new port under construction at Dunleary, the developing town's name was dropped in favour of Kingstown in his honour. The *Lightning* too received a name change owing to the presence of His Majesty on her graceful decks, becoming the *Royal Sovereign*.

Captain John MacGregor Skinner was a man much respected in the town and was a familiar sight with his pet raven on his shoulder. Born in Perth-Amboy in New Jersey in 1760, he was the second son of the Attorney General for the region. He joined the Royal Navy in 1776 and served on HMS *Phoenix* during the American War of Independence, where he was injured, losing an arm. He later served in the West India Station and lost an eye before he left the navy and joined the Post Office in 1793.

The superiority of steam vessels was recognised during the winter of 1821–22. Up to 31 May 1822, their average passage had been about seven hours and a half, compared to the sailing packet's average of fifteen hours. The weather was described as being the worst for over sixty years but the performance of the steam vessels exceeded all expectations. Sailing packets ceased to be used for the mail and the last vessel to carry the mail was the *Pelham*, which remained at Holyhead with the *Montrose* and the *Countess of Liverpool*, being used as colliers.

The *Meteor*, *Royal Sovereign* and *Vixen* were transferred to Milford in 1824 when the *Aladdin*, *Harlequin* and *Cinderella* were introduced. By 1828, the coach journey from London to Holyhead was reduced to twenty-nine hours. However, despite the improvement, conditions on the passage to Ireland were wanting. In 1832, Captain Skinner told the Parliamentary Committee that the management of the Post Office was deplorable and that the ships were not good value for money. He maintained that the high fares and bad accommodation were turning people away from using the service from Holyhead.

In his evidence to the Committee, Sir Henry Parnell agreed with Skinner and suggested that the service should be operated by the Admiralty. Later that year, on 13 October, on an approach to Holyhead, Captain Skinner and the mate were washed through a bulwark when the paddle steamer *Escape* was struck with a large wave. Their bodies were not discovered for some time and the town grieved the loss of a man of seventy years of age who had given fifty-nine years of public service to his country. A monument was erected on Black Bridge overlooking the harbour in his memory. It states,

This monument was erected by his numerous friends to the memory of John Macgregor Skinner, R.N. and for 33 years captain of one of the post office packets on this station, in testimony of his virtues, and their affectionate remembrance of him in his public capacity. He was distinguished for zeal, intrepidity and fidelity. In private life he was a model of unvarying friendship, disinterested kindness and unbounded charity. MDCCCXXXII.

An inquiry of 1836 accused the Post Office of neglect and it was decided to transfer the packets to the Board of Admiralty. The following year, they were transferred and renamed *Zephyr*, *Doterel*, *Otter*, *Sprightly*, *Cuckoo* and *Gleanor*. Meanwhile, on the Irish side of the crossing, Howth was closed as a packet port on 22 January 1834, being fully replaced by Kingstown.

In 1837, the Irish Railway Commission authorised Mr Vignoles to survey a railway line from Shrewsbury to Porth Dinllaen, in the parish of Edern, south-west of Caernarfon. The following year, the Chester & Crewe Railway engaged George Stephenson to survey a line from Chester to Holyhead which would afford the 'shortest passage across the Channel'. It was suggested that the line would carry 'Irish mails, government stores, troops and ammunition and would gain a large share of the general traffic between the two kingdoms, with eventually, a portion of the trade with the West Indies and the United States.'

A survey of the line was carried out by George Stephenson in 1839. His report was favourable and the Great Holyhead Railway Company was formed with Edward Parry of Chester as one of its main promoters. A meeting with Irish members of Parliament and others was held on 4 May that year at the Thatched House Tavern in London which resolved that, 'after examining the sections of both the rival lines of Holyhead and Porth Dinllaen, and hearing the report of Mr Stephenson, the meeting was convinced that the great Holyhead line was the most practicable, expeditious, and least expensive that could be constructed for the purpose of the communication between London and Dublin'.

Rear Admiral Sir James A. Gordon and Captain Beechey were appointed to survey the relative capabilities of the ports of Holyhead, Orme's Bay and Porth Dinllaen. They reported back to the Government, who released the report on 15 April 1840, stating their 'decided opinion that, whether as regards the distance, the passage, the convenience of a station, or the expense of constructing works, Holyhead is the most fit and eligible point for the departure and arrival of packets on the eastern side of the channel'. Captain Sir George Back and Captain Fair were given the responsibility by the Admiralty to survey the different ports on the coast and report which was 'the fittest as a terminal for communicating with the Irish capital'.

They concluded that 'the bay of Holyhead seems formed by nature as a place for shelter; and if there be anything wanting to make it complete, the defect may be easily supplied, it is, therefore, our unqualified opinion that, both as to capability and position, Holyhead is unquestionably the most eligible harbour on the coast, as a port of communication with Dublin'. Sir Frederick Smith, Lt-Col. Royal Engineers, and Professor Barlow reported to the Lords of the Treasury, 'Holyhead being selected as the best port for the Dublin packets, we are of the opinion, that the best line of railway for the communication between London and Dublin is that proposed by Mr. George Stephenson, namely, by Chester and Bangor to Holyhead.'

The Government set up a Select Committee in 1842 to investigate and report on the subject of communication between Great Britain and Ireland. The Committee looked at a railway from Worcester to Portdinllaen, a line from Chester to Caernarvon to Portdinllaen and a railway from Chester to Holyhead with a bridge over the Menai Straits.

The London & Birmingham and the Grand Junction Railway companies and the Chester & Holyhead Railway appointed Robert Stephenson as engineer-in-chief and Parliamentary notices were completed. The Bill for the building of the line was taken through Parliament in 1844 by Lord Robert Grosvenor, MP for Chester, and the Hon. William O. Stanley, MP for Anglesey, work commencing on 1 March the following year.

A plan to improve the facilities at Holyhead harbour was discussed. The Admiralty suggested enclosing an area of 90 acres, with 3,300 feet of breakwater, and 2,500 feet of pier at an expense of £400,000, while Captain Beechey proposed to enclose 176 acres, with 4,500 feet of breakwater and 3,500 feet of pier at an expense of £550,000. The engineer of the docks at Birkenhead, Mr Rendell, proposed a breakwater of 5,000 feet, from Soldier's Point eastwards, to terminate at the Platter's buoy, and a pier of 7,500 from Ynys Gybi enclosing an area of 316 acres, three-quarters of a mile long, and having six fathoms and a half of water. The larger project design which was estimated as costing £700,000 was accepted by the government and the railway company in April 1846. It was to be funded by £500,000 from the Government and £200,000 from the railway company. The breakwater still remains as the longest in the United Kingdom.

The last paddle steamers ordered for the service by the Admiralty were built in 1847 at a cost of £39,000 each. The *Banshee, Caradoc, Llewellyn* and the *St Columba* were fast ships and given good sea conditions could make the crossing in slightly over four hours.

On 1 May 1848, the line was opened between Chester and Bangor and later to Holyhead. The distance from London to Holyhead by rail is 260 miles. It carried 189,067 passengers from its opening to 31 December 1848. It was estimated that the costs of the line included £1,590,000 for permanent way, tunnelling, masonry, £164,000 for stations, £286,500 for rails and sleepers, £294,150 for land, £150,000 for the Conway Bridge, and £500,000 for the Britannia Bridge giving a total construction cost of £3,084,650 for the complete project. The cost was £945,000 above budget because of the higher cost of rails, the need to purchase more land than expected, the erection of more bridges and stronger sea defences. Mr Stephenson placed the last rivet in the Britannia Bridge on 5 March 1850.

In the Act of 1832 for 'Amending the Representation of the People', Holyhead was made a borough, together with Amlwch and Llangefni to Beaumaris, which was a parliamentary constituency electing a member to serve in Westminster. In 1837, the London & Birmingham Railway stated that they would send mail through Liverpool rather than Holyhead and the following year they invited the City of Dublin Steam Packet Company to tender for the contract. Consequently, the London mail was sent via Liverpool and the Chester mail through Holyhead.

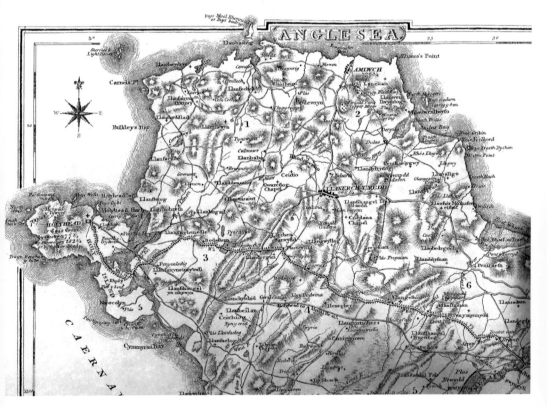

Map of Anglesey.

Building of the Britannia Bridge. (Elton Collection, Ironbridge Gorge Museum Trust)

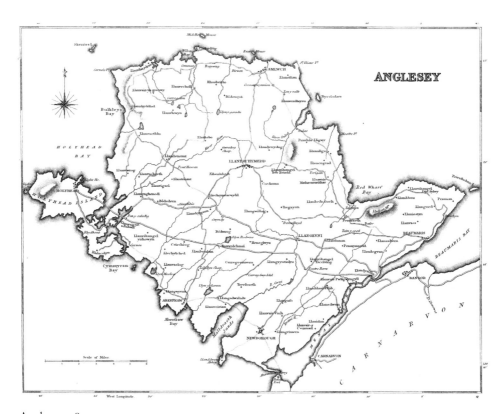

Anglesey, 1833.

3

Railway Ships

In July 1848, the Chester & Holyhead Railway was given powers to operate its own steamers after a Select Committee had concluded that the mail was conveyed at a cheaper cost by privately owned ships than on naval vessels. The company had formed a subsidiary to operate steamers from Holyhead to Kingstown and introduced the *Hibernia*, *Scotia* and *Anglia* in 1847 and the *Cambria* the following year. The vessels were flush-decked, schooner-rigged, with large paddle boxes and a clipper stern with two thin funnels forward of the bridge. They were all built of iron, the *Anglia* by Ditchburn & Mare and the *Scotia* by Wigram & Co., both having engines by Maudsley. The *Hibernia* was built by Vernon of Liverpool and engines were by C. & K. Bury and the *Cambria* was built by Laird's and fitted with Forrester engines.

The coming of the railways would greatly improve communications and, on 1 August 1848, the Admiralty packets were placed on the train, the 'Irish Mail', at London Euston at 9.45 p.m., reaching Holyhead, after transfer to road at Bangor, at 6.45 a.m. The final section of the line, across the Menai Strait to Holyhead, opened two years later. The development of the inner harbour during this period was naturally dictated by the arrival of the railway and the continued use of the port for carrying mail packets, first directly by the Government. By this time, the City of Dublin Steam Packet Company was carrying mails from Liverpool but was very much dependent for its survival upon attaining the Holyhead contract when it came up. And win it they did. From 1 January 1850, the CDSP was handed the contract to run both the day and the night mail service, much to the chagrin of the Chester & Holyhead Railway, who had invested in their new steamers and infrastructure in the expectation that they would win the contract and place the mails in the care of the railway for the entire journey from London to Dublin. The rivalry and bitterness this caused was palpable – the C&HR believing the contract to be rightfully theirs. This left the ships of the C&HR carrying passengers to Kingstown, and also cargo and cattle to North Wall in Dublin, but without the reward of the mail contract.

Initially, the C&HR developed the harbour with the CDSP, laying a tramway from the Holyhead terminus outside the town along the edge of the estuary and on to Salt Island. Horse-drawn at first, the line was later improved to allow specialised vertical boiler engines along it. It was expected that a new pier was to be erected within the Inner Harbour, and as a temporary measure to allow paddle steamers alongside the

Admiralty Pier, timber jetties were built off it. John Hawkshaw, following Rendel's death, produced different plans for a packet harbour to the north of Salt Island, to be protected by two stone piers. As a temporary measure, a timber extension was built onto the end of Admiralty Pier, and the timber jetties were replaced by a single 'L'-shaped jetty, both clearly marked as 'new jetty' and 'temporary pier' on Calver's chart of 1857. This temporary measure remained until 1863, when it was further improved and strengthened, a good direct rail link connected, and platforms erected on new timber staging. The new piers proposed by Hawkshaw were dropped.

The *Sea Nymph* and the *Telegraph* joined the railway vessels in 1856, being purchased from the Belfast Steamship Company.

The C&HR was taken over by the London & North Western Railway on 1 January 1859 and two years later they gave up their Kingstown service, concentrating on sailings to Dublin's North Wall instead, where it already operated a cargo service and had built a substantial station complete with a hotel. Their first new ship for Holyhead came out the following year. Built by Randolph, Elder & Company of Glasgow the 800 gross tons *Admiral Moorsom* was powered by two-cylinder oscillating engines, which gave her a service speed of 13 knots.

Holyhead's population of 2,132 of 1801 rose to 3,869 by 1841 and increased to 8,863 by 1851 following the construction of the railway station and the breakwater. Terraced properties were built to house the workers and their families. Holyhead Mountain saw housing developed at Llaingoch for the quarrymen. It took twenty-eight years to complete the breakwater. In May 1853, the contractors used over 400 lb of explosive in one explosion and 20,000 tons of rock were brought down. The outer harbour was made a 'safe refuge' for vessels by the construction of the mile-and-a-half breakwater and the construction of quays, cranes, sheds and cattle pens enabled the port to develop and increase its trade, enclosing an area of 316 acres.

The extension at the end of the Admiralty Pier had become known as the 'Great Eastern Jetty', presumably because this was where the *Great Eastern*, when it visited in 1859, discharged its passengers. The intention had been to set up a regular transatlantic route, but in fact the *Great Eastern* was never to return as a passenger ship. While at Holyhead, the *Great Eastern* suffered one of the strongest gales recorded, which was responsible for the sinking of the *Royal Charter* off Moelfre with a loss of over 450 passengers and crew.

The *Great Eastern*'s visit was reported in *The Illustrated London News* on 22 October 1859:

The big ship, after her trial trip dropped anchor within the breakwater at Holyhead on the afternoon of Monday week. Men-of-war and merchantmen, steam-tugs and packets, yachts, smacks and every description of craft that swims are dressed in gay colours and resounding with cheering voices. The Rock shines in the western sun and along its margin are visible a crowd of spectators. The Welsh mountains loom grandly in the background on the one side, and a broad path of sunshine stretched along the St. Georges Channel on the other. Mr. Bold, our managing director, who is also in authority over a steam-tug company at Liverpool, had ordered one of those more useful than beautiful vessels to meet us here. The *Rover* has been trying in vain to keep up with us, but now she is alongside, and in half an hour takes us ashore. The gutturals of the boatmen and porters on the pier leave no doubt that we are in Wales, but there is as little doubt that they are glad, with right hearty Welsh cordiality, to see us here we fancy we could make ourselves happy enough for a few days while a mob of visitors are in possession of our big ship. The *Great Eastern* was saluted on her arrival by HMS *Hasting, Captain Mends, C.B.* and by the dapper gun-boat, *Lieutenant Eaton*, both of which vessels were at anchor inside the harbour awaiting the visit of the Queen. It was a somewhat remarkable coincidence that as the *Great Eastern* entered Holyhead the *Princess Victoria*, a first class steamer, commanded by Captain John Harrison, brother of the commander of the *Great Eastern*, was observed beating up Channel on her outward voyage from Liverpool.

The LNWR decided in 1870 to open a service from Holyhead to Greenore in Northern Ireland, with railway connections from Newry to the port. They ordered rolling stock from Crewe and built a large hotel at Greenore. The new service commenced on 1 May 1873 with a lavish reception held in one of the transit sheds at Greenore, attended by the Lord Lieutenant of Ireland, Earl Spencer, and 600 guests. The *Edith* sailed from Greenore while the *Countess of Erne* left Holyhead to inaugurate the new venture, the two ships being temporarily transferred from the Dublin run prior to the arrival of two new vessels. The *Eleanor* was built by Hawthorn Leslie & Co. on the Tyne and was fitted with engines by Robert Stephenson & Co. Her arrival at Holyhead released the *Edith* back to the Dublin crossing. Laird Brothers, at Birkenhead, delivered the *Earl Spencer* in 1874 followed by the *Isabella* in 1877, allowing the *Countess of Erne* to return to the Dublin service.

The *Eleanor* ran aground off Leestone Point, County Down, on 27 January 1881, her passengers and crew being landed at Kilkeel. The ship was declared a total loss and was replaced by the standby ship at Holyhead, the *Telegraph*. However, she also grounded in dense fog while entering Carlingford Lough on her first crossing. A near sister to the original vessels was ordered from Laird's and the second *Isabella* was delivered. Built of steel she was driven by a four-cylinder compound engine, having oscillating cylinders of 36 in and 60 in diameter by 78 in stroke with two cranks. The *Earl Spencer* and the *Isabella* were reboilered in 1884 and the three vessels operated on the service until the *Countess of Erne* was sold to the Bristol Steam Navigation Company in 1889.

His Royal Highness, Albert Edward, the Prince of Wales and the Duke of Edinburgh were present for the official opening of the Holyhead's breakwater on 19 August 1873. Guests were taken in open coaches by a steam engine to the lighthouse at the end of the breakwater where the Prince of Wales performed the ceremony. There were on average some 1,300 men working at any one time on this project between 1849 and 1852. Between 1850 and 1864, some 6,990,862 tons of stone were transported from the quarries on the mountain to be used in the construction of Britain's longest breakwater.

Meanwhile, the Stanley Sailors Home and Reading Room was opened in 1871 with accommodation for shipwrecked sailors and the Sailors Hospital was opened on Salt Island. The Fever Hospital was also built to help sailors and the people of Holyhead. The Penrhos Almshouses were established in 1866 by the Honourable W. O. Stanley and his wife Ellen, who provided twelve cottages including the row called Llaingoch for the poor of the town. On his death in 1884, he was the Lord Lieutenant of the County of Anglesey and a justice of the peace and was buried in the grounds of the parish church of St Cybi.

Repairs to the LNWR steamers were required continuously, and boilers necessitated regular renewal. The CDSP had the use of the former Government dockyards on Salt Island, and so the LNWR established its own workshops on the north side of the harbour on the site of the old customs house and alongside Pelham Quay. In 1857, these consisted of two buildings, a smithy and a workshop, the former containing six forges, the latter a mixture of lathes, drilling machines, borers, timber steamer, and circular saw driven by a 16-hp engine. This was quickly developed into a larger establishment capable of supplying full maintenance needs for the LNWR, and remained in use into the second half of the twentieth century.

4

The New Harbour and War

With the Admiralty Pier occupied by the CDSP packet steamers, the LNWR became increasingly concerned at the lack of facilities for its ships on the services to Dublin and Greenore. Regardless of the fact that the port was government-owned the company took the decision to place orders for new and larger ships and, significantly, to improve the inner harbour, the goal being to gain the mail contract when it came up for renewal in 1883.

An Express Daylight Service was commenced in 1876 using the paddle steamers *Rose* and *Shamrock*, and this was joined in 1880 by a night service with the *Lily* and *Violet*. Initially the improvements were concentrated upon the north side of the harbour, where a new quay and large new shed were built. Land was also purchased on the south side of the harbour, a new harbour wall erected, and the coast filled in behind. Upon this were built a second large shed and storage facilities, whilst at the east end a new and larger graving dock was built. Two steam engines were installed to operate dock hydraulics and empty the dock.

The new harbour was opened by Albert Edward, Prince of Wales, on 17 June 1880. The royal party embarked on the *Lily*, commanded by Captain Beaumont and, as she sailed out of the Inner Harbour, the naval vessels present fired salutes. The *Lily* was joined by other steamers from Ireland and the *Snaefell* from the Isle of Man and returned to port with them. Later 1,000 guests were entertained to a luncheon in the Goods Shed, which had been transformed into a pavilion. The new 'V'-shaped harbour boasted arrival and departure railway lines on either side with undercover transfer from train to ship. The LNWR also opened a large hotel, ensuring close co-ordination between their trains, ships and hotel. On the first day, the Irish Mail arrived from London and decoupled its huge engine. The train was then drawn out on the branch line to the exposed Admiralty Pier by two saddle-tank engines to embark its passengers on the CDSP mailboat. But the Irish Day Express unloaded its passengers in the sheltered station where they walked across the platform to board the LNWR steamer.

Three years later, the railway did indeed win the mail contract, but only to cause disruption in the House of Commons led by Irish MPs! The Government was accused of handing the contract to a wealthy railway company, creating a monopoly and unfair treatment of the Irish company. After an investigation, the Government failed to win approval of the House and therefore new tenders were called for and in August 1883 the contract was back in the hands of the CDSP. The year 1883 also saw the arrival of the new cargo ship *Holyhead*, only for her to be lost following a collision after a few months in service. On 30 October, she sailed from Dublin at 8.00 p.m. with twenty-seven crew, 300 pigs, seventeen horses and four passengers on board. At 1.00 a.m., the following morning she collided with the German sailing ship *Alhambra* off South Stack. The *Alhambra* was on a voyage from Liverpool to New York and was cut in two and sank with a loss of thirteen lives. Seven others were picked up by *Holyhead*, which was also sinking, and when she was later abandoned, two of her crew were lost. The schooner *Gertrude* found the survivors in lifeboats and took them to Holyhead. A replacement to join her sister, the *North Wall*, was immediately ordered, the *Irene* coming out in 1885.

The *Banshee* was ordered in 1884 from Laird's yard at Birkenhead, the last paddle steamer for the LNWR. Her main saloon was sixty-four feet long and extended the full width of the ship. The first class sleeping accommodation was on the deck below, arranged in both state rooms and open berths in a large cabin, while all the second class accommodation was on the lower deck forward of the machinery spaces. The *Lily* and the *Violet* were re-boilered in 1891 and triple-expansion engines were installed, capable of developing over 4,000 ihp at 35 rpm, and when fitted to the *Banshee* in 1894 she achieved a speed of 21 knots on trials.

In 1895, the *Rosstrevor* was delivered for the Greenore service. Built by Denny's she was a twin-screw, single-funnelled steamer with two mast, powered by two sets of triple-expansion engines having cylinders of 19 in, 29 in and 44 in by 30 in stroke giving a speed of 18 knots.

With the arrival of the *Rosstrevor*, the *Earl Spencer* was withdrawn and sold for breaking up. A sistership, the *Connemara*, was delivered by Denny's in 1897 and the *Galtee More* the following year. The latter was powered by twin sets of four-cylinder triple-expansion engines with cylinders 19 in, 27 ½ in, 31 ½ in by 30 in stroke giving her a speed of 18 knots. When she came into service the *Isabella* was withdrawn and broken up.

Meanwhile, the first of four new identical twin-screw steamers, the *Ulster*, was delivered to the Irish company for the mail service in 1897. At twice the tonnage of the *Banshee* she had a speed of 24 knots, which allowed her a journey time of just 2 ¾ hours. The *Ulster* was soon joined by the *Connaught*, *Leinster* and the *Munster*. The mail contract was due for renewal in 1897 but on this occasion the LNWR declined to bid, instead concentrating its efforts on passenger and cargo traffic, which was steadily increasing. The *Olga* and the *Anglesey* joined the *North Wall* and *Irene* on the Dublin cargo run while the passenger service was also to receive new ships. For these the company turned to Wm Denny & Brothers of Dumbarton and, in late 1897, they delivered the *Cambria*, the first of four sisters. They were designed with low flush-decked hulls, slight sheer and well-proportioned and shapely counter sterns, two funnels with cowls and two masts. They were 1,842 gross tons and were fitted with four-cylinder, triple-expansion, fast-running engines giving a total of 9,000 ihp. Steam was supplied at 160 psi from eight single-ended, coal-fired boilers giving a speed of 21 knots.

The new vessels carried first and third class passengers with the whole of the first class accommodation located on the main deck. Third class was aft of the main and lower decks with the ships benefited from ventilation and electric light. The *Cambria* was delivered on 15 December 1897, the *Hibernia* on 2 February 1900, the *Anglia* on 2 May 1900 and finally the *Scotia* on 23 April 1902.

The Duke and Duchess of York travelled on the *Connaught* on 10 April 1899 and returned on the *Ulster* on the 24th of the same month. The *Ulster* was commanded by Captain John

Thomas and, although the sea was rough, the passage on each occasion was two hours and forty minutes. Captain Thomas was familiar with the mail packets constructed for the Holyhead service. He retired in October 1903 and died on 14 July 1906.

The *Eleanor* was nominated as the railway's reserve vessel at Holyhead and was employed for special excursions. She was carrying 750 Irish harvesters when she was in collision with the *Connemara* on a record low tide. The *Connemara* also collided with the *Eleanor* on 23 June 1900 when she was steaming around the outer breakwater. There were no injuries or loss of life and the *Eleanor* continued on her journey while the *Connemara* returned and transferred her passengers and cargo to the *Galtee More*. In 1902, the *Eleanor* was sold. The *Rathmore* was delivered on 3 March 1908 and was fitted with reciprocating engines with twin sets of four-cylinder triple-expansion engines of 25 in, 37 in, 41 in and 41 in by 30 in stroke. After the *Rathmore* was introduced, it was decided to convert the *Rosstrevor* to a cargo ship. On 20 March 1910, the *Connemara* was in the wars again when she collided with the *Marquis of Bute* on a voyage from Greenore to Holyhead near the Skerries. Although the *Marquis of Bute* sank within minutes, all of her crew were successfully transferred to the *Connemara*.

The *Greenore* was delivered in 1912, becoming the first turbine steamer owned by the company. Her foremast was stepped further back than the *Anglia*'s in order to clear the cargo hatch and her two funnels were fitted close together. Over her years in service she became famous for the amount of black smoke she belched out when leaving port. An order for another vessel for the route was placed with William Denny in 1914 but work did not proceed on this ship after the declaration of war.

Meanwhile, a battle of wills was raging between the Dublin Port & Docks Board and the LNWR over dues and dredging. Things eventually came to a head in 1908 when the Board raised the port dues on the LNWR's ships and the railway took this as an excuse to abandon passenger services to the North Wall and return to Kingstown. The CDSP protested the return of the prodigal operator to Kingstown on 1 April by blockading the Carlisle Pier berths with three ships! Fines were issued to the Masters concerned and even short periods in custody were administered. The political outcry was immense with Ireland's Sinn Féin calling on the people of Ireland to rally to the support of the CDSP by blacking the LNWR ships. The latter prevailed, however, and was able to secure its right to run steamers into Kingstown by way of the fact that its predecessor, the Chester & Holyhead Railway, had operated its service to Kingstown in the last century and this gave the railway the right to do so again.

The uneasy sharing of Kingstown continued until 1914 when, on the outbreak of war, the Admiralty requisitioned all four railway vessels, which were converted by the Marine Department at Holyhead into armed boarding steamers. Each was fitted with three Hotchkiss 6-pounders, the process of conversion only taking ten days, after which they sailed on war service. Under the terms of the mail contract, the CDSP ships were initially exempt from requisition and so their Kingstown service continued as the principal service to Ireland. The LNWR responded by reducing the Greenore service and transferring the *Rathmore*, the *Greenore* and the *Galtee More* south, running not to Kingstown where they would have been pitched against the high-profile mail steamers, but to Dublin alongside the *Slievemore* and the *Slieve Bawn*.

Masters were under orders from the Admiralty to steam at full speed without lights during this period. On 14 March 1918, the *Rathmore*, on a crossing from Dublin to Holyhead, collided with a troopship. Passengers and troops were transferred to a patrol vessel and she was safely towed back into port. The *Slieve Bloom* was in a collision with an American destroyer, off South Stack on 31 March, and all passengers and crew were successfully transferred to the American vessel. Meanwhile, the *Anglia* was sent by the Admiralty to Scapa Flow and joined the Grand Fleet attached to the Commander-in-Chief. She survived the hostilities and was paid off and converted to a hospital ship operating between France and Dover. While on this service, she carried King George V home after he had been inspecting troops in France. On 17 November 1915, on a voyage to Dover, she struck a mine, laid by UC 5, and sank in fifteen minutes. Eighty lives were lost but 300 of the wounded and thirty-one of her crew survived.

The *Cambria* was sent to the Grand Fleet and was in company with the 2nd Battle Squadron when the battleship *Audacious* was sunk by a mine laid by the *Berlin*. She was paid off in July 1915 and converted to a hospital ship joining the *Anglia* at Dover. She was eventually moved to Holyhead in her capacity as a hospital ship in May 1917 but was converted to an armed transport later that year and based at Dover again. She returned to Holyhead in February the following year as an armed transport vessel.

The *Hibernia* had been renamed HMS *Tara* and was placed on patrol duties at the northern end of the North Channel. On 11 March 1915, the armed merchant cruiser *Bayano* of the 10th Cruiser Squadron was torpedoed and sank in four minutes, eight of her crew being picked up by the *Tara*. In October that year, the ship was transferred to the Mediterranean to join the Western Section of the Egyptian Coast Patrol under the command of Captain R. S. Gwatkin-Williams, RN. On 5 November, she was torpedoed by U 35 and sank in eight minutes. Seventy of her crew were saved but twelve were lost. The survivors were handed over to the Senussi tribe and marched out into the desert where they suffered starvation and disease. After 364 days, they were rescued by the Yorkshire Yeomanry, led by the Duke of Westminster with a fleet of armoured cars. In August 1919, sixty-five of the survivors visited the Duke at his home in Chester and presented him with a silver model of an armoured car.

The *Scotia* joined Admiral Barlow's command and was employed on the southern section of the North Channel patrol until July 1915 when she was transferred to the eastern Mediterranean. On 10 August, she picked up Lt Holbrook and several of his crew who had been wounded near Bardia. The *Scotia* took his vessel in tow to Alexandria, some 240 miles away. She was later employed in the Red Sea and returned to Britain in May 1917 for service from Dover to France as a troopship. She was hit by a bomb at Calais on 18 July 1918 but was repaired and returned to service. On 3 November 1916, the *Connemara* sailed from Greenore to Holyhead in a strong south-westerly gale with fifty-five passengers, thirty-one crew, eighty-eight head of cattle and two horses on board. She had not progressed far when she crossed the head of the incoming steam collier *Retriever*, nearing the end of her passage from the Mersey. Neither ship could take avoiding action in the conditions and a collision occurred at the eastern end of the approach to Carlingford Lough. The *Connemara* was sliced open and within five minutes she sank with the loss of all aboard. The *Retriever* foundered fifteen minutes later with the loss of eight crew members. James Boyle, a seaman from the *Retriever*, was the only survivor of the incident. When the *Galtee More* arrived in Carlingford Lough from Holyhead, she reported a sighting of what her officers believed to be a surfaced submarine. Their 'submarine' was in fact the *Connemara* lying on her side. At the official inquiry into the loss it was stated that the *Retriever*'s navigation lights had been extinguished by the wind and sea and that it had not been possible to relight them on account of the appalling weather.

The only other major incident that took place on the Greenore service involved the *Rosstrevor*, which was on a voyage to Holyhead on 3 May 1918 when a submarine fired a torpedo at her. Fortunately, it missed and she was able to continue her voyage. At the end of the war, the *Cambria* and the *Scotia* were overhauled and returned to service at Holyhead as the *Arvonia* and the *Menevia* respectively. However, the CDSP had lost two steamers; the *Connaught*, which had been requisitioned by the Admiralty, was torpedoed and sunk in the English Channel with the loss of three crewmen, and the tragedy of the *Leinster* just northeast of the Kish Light on 10 October 1918, just a few weeks before the end of the war.

Sailing that morning from Kingstown, the *Leinster* had a crew of seventy-seven, drawn from both the Irish port and Holyhead. Also on board were twenty-two postal sorters from Dublin Post Office, working in the ship's on-board postal sorting room. There were 180 civilian passengers: men, women and children. But the majority of the ship's complement were troops, bringing the total number on board to 771. All but one of the postal sorters were killed. The Master, Captain Birch, and thirty-six of his crew were also lost. Of the passengers, 115 were killed. In total, 529 people lost their lives. The great-grandfather of one of the authors, Seaman John Merrigan, survived. Unable to recover from these losses, the CDSP left Holyhead and passed into the annals of history in 1924. Over time, their extensive maintenance workshops on Salt Island and the timber pier there both fell into disuse, the latter to be removed in 1935, when many of the workshops were also dismantled.

The crew of *Galtee More*.

Opening of the new harbour by Albert Edward, Prince of Wales, on 17 June 1880.

Holyhead Station – 'Departure of the up-boat express'.

The *Hibernia* of 1900 sailing from Holyhead.

The station clock and harbour at Holyhead. (Ian Collard Collection)

The *Scotia* of 1902.

5

Mail, Wars and Nationalisation

Anticipating their rival's problems and, with the mail contract once again going to tender, the LNWR ordered four new steamers for their resumed Kingstown service: two in operation, one on standby and one for relief duties. The contract covered two sailings a day in each direction, including Sundays, and stipulated that the time of passage to or from the Admiralty Pier at Holyhead be 2 hours 45 minutes, or 2 hours 55 minutes from the station. The time for the transfer of mails from train to ship was not to exceed 30 minutes at night and 25 minutes by day at Holyhead and 15 minutes at night and 10 minutes by day at Kingstown. If a ship failed to sail following the arrival of the mail train, a penalty of £20 for every complete hour delay would be imposed.

Denny's were again chosen to build this next generation of vessels. The first was the *Anglia*, followed by the *Hibernia*, *Cambria* and then the *Scotia*. They were twin-screw steamers of 3,467 gross tons and were powered by single-reduction-geared turbines of 16,000 shp, fed by nine coal-fired water-tube boilers, which gave them a speed of 25 knots. They were registered to carry 1,505 passengers in two classes; 936 in first and 569 in third class. Because of the length of these vessels, they were unable to swing in the Inner Harbour and had to leave stern first. Therefore they were fitted with a bow rudder and stern bridge.

The *Anglia* commenced service operating with the *Curraghmore*, which had been temporarily transferred from the Greenore route. On 27 November 1920, the *Munster* carried the last mail under the contract with the CDSP. The first mail carried by the railway company was on the *Anglia*'s sailing at 0350 from Holyhead the following day. The *Curraghmore* sailed light to Kingstown after the *Anglia* had left in order to take the mail sailing from the Irish port at 8.50 a.m. that morning. She remained on the service until the arrival of the *Hibernia* when she returned to the Greenore run.

On 1 January 1923, the LNWR became part of the London Midland & Scottish Railway. Rationalisation was the order of the day and the *Anglia* was surplus to requirements. She was transferred to Barrow for lay up in 1924 and was broken up at Troon ten years later. A skylight from the ship survives today in a private residence in Holyhead. The whereabouts of a beautiful stained-glass window from the ship's saloon and bearing the name *Anglia* is unknown. It was last seen on temporary display at Holyhead's maritime museum during the mid-1980s.

A fourth vessel was, however, required on the route at peak holiday times and the *Duke of Abercorn* (ex-*Curraghmore*) was used for this purpose. The *Duke of Abercorn* survived until 1935 when she was broken up. While passenger services to Kingstown, which had reverted to its Irish name of Dun Laoghaire in 1921, were scaled back, the LNWR's cargo service to Dublin also suffered through the effect of new customs requirements into Ireland.

On 14 January 1923, the *Hibernia* broke adrift from her moorings at the Admiralty buoy in Holyhead but the *Rosstrevor* managed to get a line on board and was able to tow her to safety.

Competition from the Heysham–Belfast route and the general civil unrest in Ireland caused the LMS to cease passenger sailings on the Greenore route in 1926. Instead a weekly cargo service was offered and this lasted until 1951. The *Rosstrevor*, *Galtee More* and the *Greenore* were all sold for breaking up, while the *Rathmore* was employed on the Tilbury–Dunkirk service in 1927 as the *Lorrain*. She was broken up in 1932.

The cattle trade had always formed a considerable part of the railway's operations and as such their cargo vessels were primarily built for shipment of livestock. For this service the company placed a £93,463 order with Denny's in 1929 for the first in what would be a class of four ships to join the reciprocating steamer *Slieve Donard* of 1921. The new vessels each offered capacity for approximately 640 head of cattle.

Entering service in 1930, the *Slieve Bloom* was a ship of innovation being equipped with electrically operated cranes and Brown hydroelectric steering. In the engine room, instead of the reciprocating steam engines that had served the port's cargo fleet for so long, a pair of compound steam turbines with single reduction gearing were installed. She was followed in 1932 by a sister, the *Slieve More*. A third and slightly different vessel, the *Slieve League*, arrived in 1935 and she was followed in 1936 by the final ship in the range for Holyhead, the *Slieve Bawn*.

In 1932, the *Hibernia*, *Cambria* and the *Scotia* were refitted and modernised enclosing some 54 feet of the promenade deck from the forward end and a lounge was added below the bridge. When the British & Irish Steam Packet's new *Leinster* and *Munster* were introduced to the Dublin to Liverpool service in 1938, it was decided to order three new 5,000-gross-ton turbine vessels for the Holyhead route from the Fairfield Shipbuilding & Engineering Company Limited. However, on the outbreak of war, the orders were cancelled and the existing fleet continued to operate.

The *Hibernia* was in trouble in August 1938 when in dense fog she was in collision with an anchored Manchester Liners ship right where the railway vessels made their swing having come astern out of the inner harbour at Holyhead. Damage to the passenger ship was slight and she was able to continue in service until repairs were made the following week, but the cargo ship lost some 120 feet of hull plating. In the same week, on 7 August, the *Cambria* was in collision with the trawler *Alcazar* with a more tragic outcome. The *Cambria* had been scheduled to leave Holyhead at 2.55 a.m., but she was fifty-four minutes late, finally getting away at 3.49 a.m. with 1,390 passengers, eighty crew and about forty tons of mails. When she left Holyhead, the weather was clear and off the South Stack Lighthouse a course was set of N 80½ W magnetic. The Master then left the bridge to attend to other duties leaving the Chief Officer in charge, a man at the wheel, a standby Quartermaster, a lookout on both port and starboard sides of the bridge and a lookout forward in the forecastle head. The vessel proceeded on her course at full speed of about 22 knots.

At 4.45 a.m., the *Cambria* ran into fog with visibility a half to three-quarters of a mile. The engines were rung to stand by, all watertight doors were closed, the fog signal commenced to be blown at regular intervals of a minute to a minute and a half and the Master went on the bridge. When the engines were rung to stand by, normal top boiler pressure of 200 lb was allowed to fall back 25–30 lb and, as a consequence, the speed of the vessel was reduced to about 20 knots.

The fog became more dense until visibility was less than 200 yards. At 5.16 a.m., the engines had made 20,000 revolutions and this was signalled from the engine room and regarded, as customary, as the halfway point and the watches commenced to change over. Before the relief was complete and with the Second Officer now also on the bridge, those on the *Cambria* heard one whistle of the *Alcazar*. Then they saw her masthead and starboard lights practically ahead and only 50 to 60 yards distant, and, although the Master ordered the wheel hard-a-starboard and rang the telegraph to full astern starboard engine, there was no time for any action to be taken before the ship ran her stem into the starboard side of the trawler. It was then 5.20 a.m. and daylight was breaking. The *Alcazar* was not seen again. The *Cambria* stood by and lowered a boat and rescued three survivors. She had had a crew of nine and one passenger, a boy of fourteen – seven were lost, including the mate.

The *Cambria* received serious bow damage and had to retire to Barrow for repairs, leaving only the *Scotia* in service. Why these repairs were not carried out at Holyhead we have been unable to ascertain – perhaps because the *Hibernia* was also under repair – but we do know that in her place came the chartered Isle of Man Steam Packet Company vessel *Victoria*.

Just after the outbreak of war, the *Scotia* was requisitioned by the Admiralty and she left Holyhead in December 1939. Under the command of Captain W. H. Hughes, the ship was ordered to Dover on 27 May 1940 on a two-hour standby for the evacuation of troops from Dunkirk. On her first run over she berthed on the East Pier at 1.30 a.m. on 29 May, where she took on over 3,000 exhausted British troops and brought them home safely to Dover. Her second run began early on 1 June. She was attacked by the German air force on passage to Dunkirk and during her run in she was struck by what was believed to be a torpedo. Fortunately, it failed to explode and no damage was done. Subsequently, the skills of Captain Hughes, Chief Officer Evan R. Pritchard (father of two future Holyhead masters, Idwal and Glynne Pritchard) and crew enabled a successful navigation through several wrecks and she was able to berth at the West Mole at about 11.00 a.m. Here, she took on board over 2,700 French troops. On departure she was attacked by twelve German aircraft and was hit by three bombs, one of which destroyed the wireless cabin. Then came a fourth and fatal bomb, which plunged down the after funnel before exploding in the engine room. Thirty-four members of the ship's crew died as a result of the attack, several more were injured, and up to 300 of the French troops she was carrying also lost their lives. Damage was so extensive that the *Scotia* soon sank. Her Master was later awarded the DSC for gallantry. In 1986, Captain Hughes celebrated his hundredth year in style. In a ceremony held aboard the *St Columba*, Captain Len Evans presented him with a beautiful oil painting.

Back on the Irish Sea, the *Cambria* figured in a dive-bombing and machine-gun attack by a German aircraft near the Kish Lightship in December 1940. The crew, led by Captain Albert Marsh, saw the raider coming out of the clouds six points on the port bow. Crossing ahead of the ship, it then turned and came down in a shallow dive to release a torpedo. Captain Marsh gave the *Cambria* a full turn, the torpedo missing and falling into the sea along the port side. Another two aerial torpedoes were fired, one from mast height, both missing thanks to a fine display of seamanship. The aircraft then strafed the *Cambria*'s decks with machine-gun fire. The third officer, Mr Jones, was hit in the thigh by a heavy-calibre bullet, dying from his injuries in the cabin of Chief Officer Evan R. Pritchard – himself fresh from the Dunkirk episode. Accurate anti-aircraft fire by the *Cambria*'s crew saw the raider off, flying very low, obviously in difficulties and believed hit.

Later, the *Cambria* moved to the Heysham–Belfast service to maintain the link in the absence of that route's ships, which had been requisitioned for war duties. With the fleet under pressure and refitting long overdue, the *Hibernia* found herself taking water one morning alongside the Carlisle Pier. She was hurriedly sailed to dry dock in Dublin where her bow plates were reinforced with concrete to enable her to get back to Holyhead for permanent repair – the *Cambria* returning to home waters to keep things moving.

After the war, the *Princess Maud* was transferred from the Stranraer–Larne route to provide additional capacity to the two remaining Holyhead vessels in service as the *Scotia*'s replacement. She was registered to carry 1,458 passengers in two classes and was capable of a service speed of 21 knots. During the early part of the war, she had operated as a troop carrier and was extensively damaged at Dunkirk after a shell exploded in her engine room. She carried 1,360,870 troops during the war, and on D-Day she was anchored off the Normandy coast with 380 United States Army engineers and twenty tons of explosives and demolition charges.

On 1 January 1948, Britain's railways were nationalised and at Holyhead the operations now came under British Railways, London Midland Region, of the new British Transport Commission (BTC). Each region within the new organisation had its own Marine Superintendent, who reported to the Chief Officer (Marine) of the Railway Executive; at least that was the case until 30 September 1953, when the Executive was abolished. From then on, the Chief Officer (Marine) came under the office of the BTC's Traffic Advisor.

Shortly afterwards, the introduction of the motorships *Hibernia* and *Cambria* completed the earlier proposal to replace the 1920-built ships of the same name with two turbine steamers from the Clyde yard of Fairfield Shipbuilding & Engineering Co. Ltd, an order subsequently cancelled due to the onset of war. After the war, BR turned to Harland & Wolff Ltd at Belfast for the two ships and the first of these, the *Hibernia*, arrived in Holyhead for the first time on 5 April 1949 to a considerable welcome from locals and dignitaries, including Lady Megan Lloyd George.

The *Hibernia* commenced service on 14 April 1949, with Captain Albert Marsh in command. Described in the April and May 1949 issues of *The Motor Ship* as being the fastest and largest British cross-channel motorships they each had a gross tonnage of 4,972 tons and were powered by 10,000 bhp, Burmeister & Wain oil engines to give a speed of 21 knots. In practice, 18 knots was sufficient to maintain the nightly service in each direction. On the *Hibernia*'s delivery passage south to Holyhead an emergency stop trial demonstrated that full power astern from full ahead had the vessel proceeding astern in just one minute and fifty-five seconds.

Her designers certainly had their work cut out for them, having to cater for both day and night passages during the summer season. Therefore, the *Hibernia*, and of course the *Cambria*, had to be arranged for both purposes. Accommodation was provided for 2,361 passengers in first and third classes. In first class, 166 passengers were accommodated in single and two-berth cabins in addition to two open-berth rooms for fifty-six people. Four special cabins were included, with private bathrooms. For third class passengers, there were two- and four-berth cabins for 154, with the two open-berth rooms accommodating sixty. On the Boat Deck (A) were the cabins for the Master, deck officers and engineers and also eight first class cabins, an entrance to the first class accommodation being on this deck. Below, on the Promenade Deck (B), was a large main first class lounge in the forward part of the deckhouse, leading aft to the first class smoke room with the third class smoke room adjoining. Spacious entrances for both classes were also located on the Upper Deck (C) as were a considerable number of single and two-berth cabins. Below, on the Main Deck (D), were two dining saloons for both classes besides further lounges. The stewards had their cabins at the forward end of the Main Deck while the seamen were located aft. Below the Main Deck, the Lower Deck was mainly a cabin deck with first class cabins forward and third class aft. The open-berth rooms were also on this deck.

Each ship was divided into eleven watertight compartments by ten watertight bulkheads. The double bottom was divided for fresh water, water ballast, oil fuel and lubricating oil. The forward and aft peaks were arranged for water ballast. Forward of the machinery space deep tanks were provided for oil fuel and for fresh water, while aft of the machinery space were deep tanks for oil fuel or water ballast and for fresh water. There were two cargo holds and tween decks forward for the shipment of general cargo and cars, a tween deck space aft, and one of the tween decks forward being arranged alternatively for the carriage of cargo or passengers. Large mail and baggage rooms were located on the Main Deck aft and for each class of passenger baggage rooms were provided.

The *Cambria* arrived in her home port from Harland & Wolff's Belfast yard on 5 May 1949. The old *Hibernia* and *Cambria* were withdrawn from service in December 1948 and May 1949 respectively and were broken up at Barrow and Milford Haven. During their first two years, the new ships gained a reputation for their tendency to roll but this was rectified during the 1951 refit when Denny-Brown stabilisers were fitted.

The regular pattern for the mailboats was for one nightly sailing in each direction on a year-round basis. This was increased to a second sailing in each direction during the summer months with a third at peak periods taken by the *Princess Maud*. It is appropriate here to look at how the ships were manned. Each ship had its own permanent crew who were without exception all highly qualified – the masters and officers all holding foreign-going Masters Tickets and the seniors all holding pilotage licences for Holyhead, Dublin and Belfast. Of six engineers in the engine room, the Chief, 2nd and 3rd Engineers all held Chief's Tickets with motor endorsements. The mailboat Radio Officers held First Class PMGs with Radar Maintenance. The Petty Officers and Ratings were nearly always all former Deep Sea men bringing huge seamanship skills to the port. Naturally, English was the official language on board, but Welsh was spoken widely.

And the uniforms – immaculate! There was great pride in appearance, all hands being superbly turned out. And that went for the ships too – gleaming brasswork, white wooden decks, flag etiquette and strict timekeeping, all in a day's work. The routine was for a mailboat to leave Holyhead at 3.15 a.m. and arrive in Dun Laoghaire at 6.45 a.m. This ship would then leave the Irish port at 8.45 p.m. and berth at the station arrival platform in Holyhead at 12.15 a.m. There the ship would lie overnight before shifting over on her ropes to the departure berth opposite at around 7.30 a.m. The shore gang would wash down first, and on completion of this would call the duty officer and commence the shift. The bow would be hove out to midway between the berths and held in position by a head rope and check ropes whilst the stern was pulled over. Two bow ropes were left out, as was the stern check rope, which was secured to a slip hook on the arrival berth.

Throughout the hours of daylight, maintenance would be carried out before taking up the 3.15 a.m. sailing again at the start of another forty-eight-hour cycle. Thus, each ship sailed from the Welsh port at 3.15 a.m. At sailing time, the bow was first pulled out as before and held in position whilst the stern was pulled out. A member of the shore gang stood by the slip hook, and on hearing a blast on the chief officer's ACME Thunderer mouth whistle, would smartly strike the slip hook with a hammer to release the rope. The bow ropes being let go at the same time. The stern rope would be winched back on board as quickly as possible and the 2nd Officer would signal all clear on the telegraph as the eye came out of the water. During the summer, when double sailings took place, the rope shift took place immediately the departure berth was clear. The ship then moved astern down through the inner harbour, making her way to the outer to swing. Having stopped, the Master, Chief Officer and Quartermaster would then 'Change Bridges' from the aft to the main bridge where they joined the 2nd Officer and another Quartermaster. Moving ahead, the ship rounded the breakwater and set a course west for the Kish Light. The Chief Officer, joined by the Bosun and the Carpenter would 'Make Rounds', returning afterwards to advise the Master 'all secure, Sir'. Once clear of pilotage waters, the Captain would go below for the passage and the Quartermaster would set about making toast, tea and coffee for those remaining on the bridge for the watch. The Master would come up again approaching the Kish and 'take her' from the South Burford Buoy marking the entrance to Dublin Bay while the officers prepared for stations for arrival at Dun Laoghaire. Being 'all fast' alongside the arrivals berth on the Carlisle Pier at 6.45 a.m., the passengers would go ashore where train connections to all parts of Ireland were alongside the ship. Once the mails had been discharged it was time for the crew to 'knock off' for a hearty breakfast.

Lying alongside at Dun Laoghaire all day, the ship was very much in full view of the public. The smart British Railways livery of black hull, white upperworks and black-topped buff funnel was always enhanced by the Royal Mail Pennant flying yard arm in addition to the usual flags around the ship; Red Ensign, Irish courtesy flag, Stem Jack, House Flag and Blue Peter. It was very much a local pastime to walk the piers to 'see the mailboat' sail.

Passengers boarding in Dun Laoghaire for the evening sailing were permitted to remain on board at Holyhead after arrival shortly past midnight, leaving the ship at a more sociable hour and following a hearty breakfast. Meanwhile, officers and crew not on duty were free to go home for the night – it was a condition of service that they resided in and around Holyhead.

Returning to the ship after a night's sleep ashore, the whole routine was repeated. While the ship lay in Holyhead during the day, the opposite ship lay in Dun Laoghaire. However, during the summer months, 'heavy running' meant the mailboat arriving in Dun Laoghaire at 6.45 a.m. would sail again in the morning while the other ship, having arrived in Holyhead at 12.15 a.m., would sail again the following afternoon. As for the *Princess Maud*, as standby ship, she would usually sail for Dun Laoghaire in the evenings to pick up passengers. Captain John Bakewell, who served as 2nd officer in the ship, recalls:

> We used to join her in the early evening in case we were required to sail light to Dun Laoghaire in order to pick up passengers left behind on the 8.45 p.m. sailing from there. The junior 2nd Officer would stand by the telegraph office in Holyhead and wait for the call from Dun Laoghaire as to whether the ship was wanted or not. If wanted, the officer would wave his arms to the Chief Officer keeping a lookout and very quickly she would be ready for sea.

Additionally, a very popular *Princess Maud* sailing was the 'North Wales Excursion', when she sailed from Holyhead to Dun Laoghaire at 9.00 a.m. with day-trippers from along the coast brought to the ship side by train.

One benefit of nationalisation to the port was a significant increase in work for the Marine Workshops. Holyhead boasted extensive facilities to maintain its not inconsiderable fleet of ships, and now, under the new regime, all Irish Sea, North Channel and St George's Channel ships were dry-docked and refitted at the port. On occasion, particularly in later years, ships from the English Channel services were also regular visitors to the larger of the two dry docks.

In 1950 and again in 1951, the *St Patrick* served for a short time relieving on the Dun Laoghaire run. Other ships to make brief appearances during the 1950s were the *Duke of York* and from the Channel Islands, the *Isle of Sark*. Before the end of the decade, the Isle of Man Steam Packet Company's *Snaefell* was hurriedly chartered by British Railways on 12 August 1959 to replace the *Cambria*. Leaving Douglas, Isle of Man, at 7.00 p.m., she arrived at Dun Laoghaire four hours later and sailed again for Holyhead at 11.30 p.m.

Captain Marsh retired in 1950 after a distinguished thirty-three years service at the port. A young Albert Marsh served as a sub-lieutenant on the *Hibernia*, which was requisitioned by the Royal Navy and renamed HMS *Tara* early in 1914. He was on board when she was torpedoed and sunk by the U-35. He survived the sinking and, along with the rest of the surviving officers and crew, was handed over to the Senussi tribe and marched out into the desert. During the Second World War, he commanded the *Cambria* and escaped the attention of U-boats patrolling the Irish Sea. His vessel was also bombed and shot at by the Luftwaffe on passage to Holyhead, but he successfully out-manoeuvred the aircraft.

The principal themes to have dominated the development of the port in the post-war era were changes in the mode of travel with the rise of the motor car and decline of rail use, resulting in the closure of the Station Hotel in 1955.

As far as cargo was concerned, in the old cattle ships, any type of general cargo one could think of was stowed in the hold. Shortly after nationalisation, closed containers for the shipment of fresh meat and other perishable goods were introduced. Up to sixty small containers of four tons and capacities ranging from 500 to 775 cu. ft could be shipped at any one time. The containers were categorised, some were FM containers and others were BD containers, these usually containing furniture. They were secured by wire lashings, which was carried out by the quartermasters. This method of transportation proved so successful that major improvements were put in place at the ports to meet increased demand. While new cranes were installed ashore, the ships lost their well-balanced looks as mainmasts were removed and re-stepped immediately forward of the funnel, to make way for containers on deck. With the new efficiencies of containerisation, the elderly *Slieve Donard* was withdrawn in 1954 by which time the *Slieve Bawn* was spending long periods in service on the Heysham to Belfast service alongside sister ship the *Slieve Bearnagh*. Happily, the *Slieve Donard*'s bell survives in Stena Line's Dun Laoghaire office.

In addition to carrying cattle, racehorses were also frequently shipped. The foreman ashore would ask the ship 'Will you take horses tonight?', to which the reply was given yes or no dependent on the weather forecast. If the wind was forecast to be strong to gale from the south, the Master would refuse shipment because of the excessive rolling which may be experienced. Captain Glynne Pritchard recalls,

> I have on occasion been down with the grooms, off the Stacks, 'talking' to the horses as conditions turned out to be worse than expected. It was essential that the horse stalls had wooden battens secured to the deck against which they could brace their hooves. The vet at Holyhead was very keen on this. My father Evan R. Pritchard was Master of the *Slieve Donard* in the late 1940s. They were double tripping and it was not a very pleasant night. On arrival at Holyhead the foreman shouted up from the quay, 'Will you take horses out'. My father replied, 'If I can stand up here on two bloody feet, I'm sure a horse can stand down there on four bloody feet.'

Irish Government records for 1956 indicate that livestock accounted for almost 35 per cent of Ireland's total exports. British Railways routes from Heysham, Holyhead and Fishguard handled some 37 per cent of this livestock trade.

The Shipping and International Services Department was established at the BTC in January 1957, and during the 1960s British Railways underwent a radical reorganisation, including the abolition of the BTC. The new British Railways Board (BRB) came into being on 1 January 1963 and, as part of its new image, British Railways was rebranded as British Rail, complete with a new corporate image, introduced with its double arrow logo in 1964/65.

When the *Hibernia* and the *Cambria* were fifteen years old, they returned to their builders for a major refit. New aircraft-type seats replaced distinctive post-war style furnishings in remodelled public rooms. Although more cabin berths were provided, the reduction in the number of open berths saw the overall number of berths reduced from 436 to 357. On the Upper Deck (C), cabins and staterooms were replaced by second class lounges amidships and aft. On the Main Deck (D), the cabins were replaced by a second class smoke room and a tea bar. Above, on the Promenade Deck (B), the first and second class smoke rooms were converted into a tea lounge with seating for 146 persons. The after end of the main lounge became a second class lounge with seating for 106 passengers. In addition to this, the previously open passageways aft were plated in to provide enclosed accommodation with seats alongside the casings and the ship's sides. Passenger capacity was reduced from 2,361 to 1,900.

The *Cambria*, ready at Dun Laoghaire for a summer daylight sailing to Holyhead during the late 1950s. (Justin Merrigan Collection)

A view of Holyhead from Skinners Monument. (Ian Collard Collection)

The *Scotia*, built by Denny's at Dumbarton in 1920. (Nigel Thornton Collection)

Captain W. H. Hughes. (Charles Brinsley Sheridan)

Captain Woodall on the *Hibernia*. (Charles Brinsley Sheridan)

Carlisle Pier arrival on the *Hibernia*. (Charles Brinsley Sheridan)

Carlisle Pier, Dun Laoghaire. (Charles Brinsley Sheridan)

Above left: Captain Jesse Hughes on the *Cambria*. (Charles Brinsley Sheridan)

Above right: The *Scotia* and the *Hibernia* berthed together at Holyhead. (Charles Brinsley Sheridan)

Captain Albert Marsh. (Charles Brinsley Sheridan)

The cargo vessel *Slieve League*. (Bobby Sinclair)

The *Hibernia*, leaking alongside the Carlisle Pier. (Charles Brinsley Sheridan)

The *Hibernia* leaking at Dun Laoghaire. (Charles Brinsley Sheridan)

The *Hibernia* at Dun Laoghaire on VE Day. (Charles Brinsley Sheridan)

The *Cambria* in Dublin Bay. (Nigel Thornton Collection)

ADMIRALTY PIER AND IRISH MAIL-BOAT, HOLYHEAD.

The Admiralty Pier, Holyhead. (Ian Collard Collection)

Above left: Chief Officer Evan R. Pritchard. (Charles Brinsley Sheridan)

Above right: Commander Sheil, Dun Laoghaire Harbour Master. (Charles Brinsley Sheridan)

Left: The *Cambria*'s funnels. (Charles Brinsley Sheridan)

Left: Arriving at Dun Laoghaire is the splendid *Princess Maud*. (Charles Brinsley Sheridan)

Below: The *Cambria* on speed trials in 1949. (Captain Walter Lloyd Williams Collection)

The *Cambria*. (Ian Collard Collection)

The *Hibernia* of 1949 arrives at Holyhead. (Nigel Thornton Collection)

A busy scene at Holyhead in the 1950s. (Justin Merrigan Collection)

Carlisle Pier upgrade in 1953. (Captain Simon Coate Collection)

An early 1960s postcard showing the *Hibernia* and the *Princess Maud* at Dun Laoghaire.

The Irish Mail train emerges from the Britannia Railway Bridge.

Westland Row Boat Train at Dun Laoghaire on 8 October 1960. (Ernie Brack)

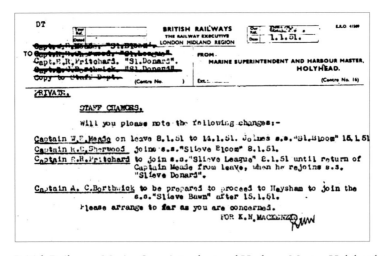

```
                                        E.R.O. 41589
LMS INTERNAL CORRESPONDENCE              |          Our Reference        Your Reference
To                                     NO  G.Pad.8/5
   Mr. E.R. Pritchard,                      From MARINE SUPERINTENDENT & HARBOUR MASTER,
   Acting Chief Officer,
   R.M.S. "Cambria".                                            HOLYHEAD
                     (Centre No.    )   EXIN                         (Centre No  16)

   DUBLIN PILOTAGE Certificate       ..... 12th January .......... 19 42
      I enclose herewith the following :-

      (1)  Pilotage Act 1913.
      (2)  Pilotage  Order Confirmation Act 1926
      (3)  Pilotage Byelaws.

      I am pleasede to congratulate you upon having
   been so successful as I understand that your marks
   were the highest in recent  records.
```

Letter to E. R. Pritchard from the Marine Superintendent and Harbour Master congratulating him on obtaining his Dublin Pilotage Certificate.

```
DT                                   BRITISH RAILWAYS           L.R.O. 41589
                                     THE RAILWAY EXECUTIVE    1.1.51.
                                     LONDON MIDLAND REGION
TO  Captain W.F.Meade "Sl.Bloom".
    Capt.E.R.Pritchard. "Sl.Donard".    FROM.
    Captain K.E.Sherwood. "Sl.Donard".  MARINE SUPERINTENDENT AND HARBOUR MASTER,
    Copy to Staff Dept.                                HOLYHEAD.
                     (Centre No.    )   Ext.             (Centre No 16)

    PRIVATE.

       STAFF CHANGES.

       Will you please note the following changes:-

    Captain W.F.Meade on leave 8.1.51 to 14.1.51. Joines s.s."Sl.Bloom" 15.1.51
    Captain K.E.Sherwood joins s.s."Slieve Bloom" 8.1.51.
    Captain E.R.Pritchard to join s.s."Slieve League" 2.1.51 until return of
                          Captain Meade from leave, when he rejoins s.s.
                          "Slieve Donard".

    Captain A. C.Borthwick to be prepared to proceed to Heysham to join the
                          s.s."Slieve Bawn" after 15.1.51.
       Please arrange to far as you are concerned.
                                      FOR K.N.MACKENZIE
```

Letter from British Railways, Marine Superintendent and Harbour Master, Holyhead, of 1 January 1951, detailing staff changes.

6

Changing Times:
Cars and Containers

The Holyhead–Dun Laoghaire route entered the car ferry age with the 1963 order for a new ship from Hawthorn Leslie (Shipbuilders) Ltd. Built at a cost of £1.6 million, she was saddled with the unimaginative name of *Holyhead Ferry I* when launched on 17 February 1965. To facilitate the new ship, extensive engineering works were carried out on both sides of the Irish Sea. At Holyhead, the Admiralty Pier berth, an area that had been little used by the port since the closure of the CDSP, was modified and provided with a linkspan. At Dun Laoghaire, things were not so straightforward and a temporary berth on the East Pier had to be constructed while plans for a more permanent solution were discussed.

Holyhead's new car ferry could accommodate 153 average-sized cars on her vehicle deck, which was equipped with a turntable forward and aft to assist with positioning cars ready for disembarkation. A small mezzanine deck forward was accessed by hydraulically operated ramps port and starboard. Two hatches were also fitted fore and aft, primarily for loading mail into the ship but also to allow cars to be lifted out should the stern door fail. Passenger capacity was 1,000 and sixty-four berths were available in a variety of cabins. Surprisingly, however, the ship was powered by steam turbine machinery. But not only that, she lacked bridge control of the engines, having electric telegraphs and, of course, was stern-loading only. All of this at a time when a ship that would see herself at Holyhead in later years as the *Earl William* was already one year old and equipped with bridge-controlled diesel engines and boasting bow and stern through loading. The contrast was stark and the comparison highlighted that British Rail did occasionally get it wrong.

The new service opened for business on 9 July 1965, not with the *Holyhead Ferry I*, which was late from her builders, but the newly converted *Normannia* from the Dover–Boulogne run. The *Holyhead Ferry I* finally took over on 19 July. During the height of the summer season, one round trip was offered daily, departing Holyhead at 10.45 a.m. and Dun Laoghaire at 3.30 p.m. At weekends, an additional round trip was offered, leaving the Welsh port at 8.15 p.m. and from Dun Laoghaire at 6.00 a.m. The whole operation was a most civilised affair. Cabins and berths for the 6.00 a.m. sailing from Dun Laoghaire were available for occupation overnight. Passengers holding cabin and berth reservations for this sailing could report with their vehicles ready for loading between 11.30 a.m. and 11.59 p.m. the previous night. The service was a rampant success but even so it was still a seasonal affair and, on 17 October, the route reverted to mail ship operation until the summer of 1966.

The arrival of the *Holyhead Ferry I* brought the withdrawal of the venerable *Princess Maud*, her final sailing from Dun Laoghaire being on 4 September 1965. Of all the Irish Sea ships, the *Princess Maud* is arguably the one most local people still speak of when reminiscing about rough winter crossings! Having no stabilisers, on a wild night she was said to be unbearable; her reputation for rolling mercilessly being well-earned. On one very bad night, the father of co-author Justin Merrigan arrived at Dun Laoghaire Pier to find not the *Cambria* or the *Hibernia* alongside, but the *Princess Maud*. He promptly turned around and went back home and made his crossing the next day! She was quickly sold for further service in Greek waters. As the *Princess Maud* left Holyhead for the final time, one of the Marine Yard fitters, Wesley Williams, who was an accomplished bugler, played 'The Last Post' as she steamed past the Sheer Legs on her way to warmer climes. Bearing the name *Venus*, and following alterations to make her suited to her new tasks, she took up her new duties in June 1966. However, after just three years she was resold for use as a shipyard accommodation vessel at Copenhagen and was finally broken up in Spain in 1973.

FIRST COST AND GROSS BOOK VALUE OF HOLYHEAD VESSELS 31/12/65

Vessel	First Cost £	Gross Book Value £
Cambria	909,545	1,210,231
Harrogate	182,796	182,796
Hibernia	904,498	1,201,042
Holyhead Ferry I	1,627,988	1,627,988
Selby	179,800	179,800
Slieve Bawn	97,550	164,223
Slieve Donard	553,740	555,650
Slieve League	84,757	87,804

No sooner had the *Princess Maud* left Holyhead than the mail service found itself in trouble bringing Heysham's *Duke of Rothesay* south for her first spell of Dun Laoghaire service between 25 September and 11 October 1965, filling in for the *Cambria*, which had come to grief on the Irish port's West Pier in dense fog. The 'Rothesay' was back again in January and February 1966 providing further relief on the mail service.

The *Slieve Bloom* was the first of the cattle boat quartet to see withdrawal and in 1965 she and the *Slieve More* were sold to Van Heyghen Freres for breaking up in Belgium. With their withdrawal, the *Slieve Bawn* was moved back to Holyhead and shortly afterwards Associated Humber Lines' *Harrogate* was transferred to the port, being adapted for the service at Immingham on completion of her North Sea duties and entering Irish Sea service on 15 April 1965. Her sisters, the *Selby* and the *Darlington*, became frequent visitors, assisting when traffic demanded additional capacity. Neither ship was a particular favourite with their Holyhead masters as they were single screw. The ship would berth port side to – the easiest side with a right-handed single propeller

– at the coal crane to discharge/load containers. Getting the bow to seaward for departure was accomplished by running a rope from the bow, outboard to a bollard astern of the ship, then after heaving the stern in as much as possible with a stern rope, heaving on the bow rope to pull her around. Arriving at North Wall it was a different story, starboard side to, and the 'fresh' in the River Liffey to contend with.

Meanwhile, having completed her first season, the *Holyhead Ferry I* took on the role of winter relief ship and, on 14 February 1966, she made her first appearance on the Stranraer–Larne service, remaining there for one month before returning to her Welsh home port. Apart from the gradual extension of her Holyhead season this routine pretty much continued for the rest of the 1960s and, during the winter of 1968/69, she found herself sailing on the mail service departing Holyhead on the time-honoured 3.15 a.m. sailing on Mondays, Wednesdays and Fridays.

The *Slieve League* followed her two sisters to Belgian breakers in February 1967, being towed there after sale for £14,000 and leaving the *Slieve Bawn* as the last of the 'old boats' until she too met her fate.

When British Rail's Freightliner block trains began in 1965, ISO (International Standards Organisation) and the container revolution had barely begun. The original intention was for a purely domestic Freightliner rail service – no consideration being given to the possibility of continuing the operation across the sea. That, however, soon changed. The first (ISO) 20-foot containers were shipped through Holyhead for the first time on 2 January 1968. In preparation for this, the *Harrogate* and the *Selby* were both converted to cellular container ships. Across the country, at Harwich, British Rail launched its Sea Freightliner service between Harwich and Zeebrugge with the purpose-built cellular container ships *Seafreightliner I* and *Seafreightliner II*. Plans were soon put in place for an equivalent full service on the Irish Sea and an order for two similar ships was placed with the Irish yard of Verolme Dockyard in Cork. In the meantime, the *Isle of Ely* was converted to cellular operation and transferred from the North Sea to Holyhead, joining the *Harrogate*, the *Selby* and the *Darlington*.

The year 1969 saw the passing of a hardworking Holyhead stalwart, the *Pick Me Up*. Built by Fleming & Ferguson Ltd in 1902, she was a grab dredger and hopper and, working eight hours a day, five days a week, she was used to maintain the depth of the Inner Harbour. She was powered by a two-cylinder compound engine, which drove a single screw and was fitted with a Priestman crane. She was delivered to Pounds at Portsmouth for breaking up in April 1969.

July 1968 brought another car ferry to the Dun Laoghaire service: the Stranraer-based *Caledonian Princess*. This ship operated alongside the *Holyhead Ferry I* until 5 September. Between 1969 and 1975, having had side-loading doors cut into her vehicle deck, the ship was mainly associated with the Fishguard–Rosslare service but by and large, since leaving Stranraer, she led something of a nomadic career often acting as support or substitute for other members of the fleet.

In 1969, Dun Laoghaire's new IR£850,000 St Michael's Wharf car ferry terminal was opened by the *Holyhead Ferry I* on 14 March. Capable of handling 650 cars a day, the new 175-metre-long pier offered linkspans on both sides of the terminal. While this meant that two vessels could berth simultaneously, the principal purpose was to permit a ship to lie on the more sheltered side of the pier. The controversial temporary terminal on Dun Laoghaire's East Pier was closed that year and, in four years of operation, 95,000 cars had been landed at the site. Meanwhile, the establishment of an aluminium smelter at Holyhead by Rio Tinto Zinc in the late 1960s saw the construction of a new pier off Salt Island linked to the plant by an underground conveyor belt for importing the ore, and an increase in port facilities to handle the finished product.

The new cellular container ships, *Brian Boroime* and *Rhodri Mawr*, came out in 1970. Named after an Irish and a Welsh monarch respectively, it was a little-known fact that the 'Brian' seemed to have been saddled with an incorrect spelling of her name. In the Irish language some consonants can undergo a transformation called séimhiú (pronounced Shea-Vu). In the old Irish script, this was shown by putting a dot above the letter. Modern Irish is printed using the standard Western alphabet, and the dot has been replaced by the letter 'h' following the consonant. The 'M' of Boroime appeared to have neither a dot over it, or an 'H' after it to give the correct Boroimhe, pronounced Bor-oy-va – or so it seemed! At a reunion of Sealink staff in Holyhead in August 2006, the *Brian Boroime*'s former Chief Engineer, Eric March, informed co-author Justin Merrigan that the séimhiú was in fact in place, in the form of a raised weld mark. However, it always seemed to escape the painter's attention during each dry-docking – much to his frustration!

At Holyhead, on the east side of the inner harbour, occupying berths 5 & 6, the new Freightliner Terminal was equipped with two 30-ton Wellman Transport cranes for ship-to-shore movements and two 30-ton Goliath cranes for rail-to-road transfer. The storage capacity of the terminal was around 700 TEUs (Twenty-foot Equivalent Units) with customs clearance available on the spot. Sealink's own fleet of lorries and trailers fed the cranes and ship discharge/loading rates of over thirty containers per hour were the norm. The new Freightliner Terminal at Dublin Port had an area of 3.25 hectares. From here, a late afternoon sailing operated Monday to Friday linking into the UK's Freightliner network. The berth offered six metres at its lowest tide and was served by two 30-ton cranes. The storage area was also equipped with two 30-ton Goliaths. Altogether, up to 495 containers could be stored in a mix of six-, nine- and twelve-metre boxes. A similar terminal was put in place at Gotto Wharf in Belfast.

Holyhead received a significant setback in 1970. Robert Stephenson's Britannia Bridge across the Menai Strait was virtually destroyed in a fire. This was accidentally started on 23 May by boys searching for bird nests and using lighted newspaper as torches, severing Anglesey's rail link with the mainland. The lining of the bridge was highly flammable being of old railway sleepers coated with creosote. The fire was so intense that the wrought-iron tubes buckled, necessitating the rebuilding of the bridge. BR chartered the *Kingsnorth Fisher* to operate three sailings from Holyhead to Barrow in mid-June to retrieve eleven trapped locomotives. With no way of connecting the mailboats, it was decided to transfer the mail and the new ISO service to Heysham. With an extended crossing time of 7 hours and 30 minutes, the *Hibernia* and the *Cambria* continued to sail from Heysham to Dun Laoghaire until 31 January 1972, when they were welcomed back to Holyhead with a fireworks display and what seemed like the whole town lining the quays to witness the event.

Helping out the mailboats as relief ship during this time was the Fishguard stalwart *St David*. She was transferred to Holyhead at the end of 1969 having been replaced on St George's Channel by the *Caledonian Princess*. Prior to her disposal she too found herself sailing between Heysham and Dun Laoghaire.

The *Lord Warden*, England's first purpose-built, stern-loading car ferry, made her first appearance at Holyhead in 1971, spending that summer in operation to Dun Laoghaire. The ship had a vehicle deck open to the elements at the stern and protected only by a set of gates. Glynne Pritchard recalls serving on the ship as Chief Officer with Captain Len Evans and with much cause for concern being frequently sent aft to check that all was well. Eighteen years previously, the *Princess Victoria* was overwhelmed during a storm in the North Channel when her similar stern gates were breached.

The popular Captain 'Richie' Roberts retired in 1971. First going to sea in 1922, he came to Holyhead in 1939 as 2nd Officer. During the war years, he was primarily on the *Hibernia*. In 1947, he was transferred to Heysham–Belfast route. He returned to Holyhead as Chief Officer on the *Slieve Donard* in 1949, and in 1954 became a Master on the cargo ships. In 1960, Captain Roberts gained his first passenger command – the *Princess Maud*. In 1965, after forty-three years at sea, he became the first Master of the *Holyhead Ferry I*.

When the *Rhodri Mawr* and *Brian Boroime* were finally able to enter service from Holyhead to Dublin and Belfast, traffic volumes grew rapidly, reaching their highest-ever annual total of 73,000 containers in 1973. The *Colchester* was transferred from Harwich to Holyhead in 1972. A year later, she was tried on the Heysham–Belfast run but this was short-lived and soon after she was laid up at Holyhead until sold for Mediterranean service in 1975. The arrival of the *Colchester* saw the end of the old *Slieve Bawn*. Initially sold to A. King, Norwich, she was quickly resold to Metalexport of Beirut. However, she then went to Spanish shipbreakers and left Holyhead on 15 June 1972, arriving at Gijon ten days later.

In 1973, the *Holyhead Ferry I* had her first spell of English Channel service after which she relieved Fishguard's *Caledonian Princess* for annual overhaul. By now, the 'Ferry I' found herself based at Dover with that port's *Dover* being based at Holyhead! The reason was the latter's greater car capacity over her half-sister.

The late Captain Len Evans recalled a voyage in the *Dover* in September 1974.

We left Holyhead in flat calm conditions, but it was a good Force 12 Northerly in Dun Laoghaire. I was able to berth, but the sea in the harbour was such that she was pitching and rolling alongside the berth.

Clearly she was going to suffer major damage, and so I sailed back out into Dublin Bay where I turned circles for the next twelve hours until conditions improved slightly and I was able to go back alongside, discharge cars and passengers and reload.

At about 11.00 p.m. I had a message from Valley that the wind was now 83 mph. Coming into Holyhead was not funny; at one stage it seemed inevitable that she would smash into the Refit Berth. However, she came around, and I was delighted to berth in the Station Berth.

After we got alongside, the Carpenter came up to my room, which he never did usually and said, 'Captain, if I was to die, I prayed for you, and she came around', with tears rolling down his cheeks. He left me a very chastened man, that one of my crew had thought so much!

The *Duke of Rothesay* was also back at Holyhead in 1973, this time after her conversion to a stern-loading car ferry. The ship spent much time between Heysham, Holyhead and Fishguard in a relief role but her days were numbered. Replaced by her sister, the *Duke of Lancaster*, in July 1975, the 'Rothesay' was sold for scrap at Faslane, leaving Holyhead under tow in October of that year.

Holyhead's Senior Master, Captain Will Roberts retired in 1973. Starting his seagoing career as an apprentice on a tramp steamer in 1928, he joined the Holyhead ships in 1940, his first command being the *Slieve Donard*. Captain Roberts spent twelve years in command of the *Cambria* and carried many famous celebrities including Taylor and Burton (together), James Mason, James Cagney, and Laurel and Hardy. His favourite ship was the *Princess Maud*, but speaking on retirement from the *Cambria* he remarked, 'The last ship is always the best ship!'

The skill of Holyhead crews has often been tested over the years and a magnificent display of seamanship was witnessed in 1974 when the Heysham–Belfast cargo ship *Container Venturer* suffered engine failure thirteen miles off Mew Island at the entrance to Belfast Lough. The *Duke of Lancaster* altered course to stand by the drifting ship until tugs were summoned from Belfast. With weather conditions deteriorating and the passenger ship having been released from the scene, Holyhead's *Rhodri Mawr* was tasked to stand by when the tugs failed to make contact due to the sea state. Under the command of Captain Bob Crane the 'Rhodri' found the *Container Venturer* drifting northwards. Captain Crane decided to try and take the ship in tow and, despite the conditions, he was successful. Towing commenced using the anchor cable of the *Container Venturer* and polypropylene rope from the 'Rhodri'. It took three hours to bring her into the approaches to Belfast where the tow was handed to the awaiting tugs. It was an extremely high degree of seamanship, which perhaps prevented a terrible outcome.

The end of the Dublin livestock service came in 1975; the last remaining cattle boat, the *Slieve Donard*, leaving Holyhead for the last time, under tow, on 1 July. Sold for £200,000 to Nashar Saudi Lines for service between Saudi Arabia, India and Somalia, the ship was dry-docked in Birkenhead from where, after a refit, she sailed south for the Red Sea. There was considerable outcry concerning the closure, particularly because for the year to closure the number of cattle imported through Holyhead was 80,573 – a substantial increase on the previous year. Speaking of the closure in the Houses of Parliament on 2 December, Cledwyn Hughes, MP for Anglesey, commented,

> In withdrawing this service British Rail have closed the best cattle port in the United Kingdom. I call in aid the evidence which Prof. O. G. Williams, a distinguished agriculturist, gave in September to the TUCC. He had visited Holyhead and made a detailed examination as a member of the O'Brien Committee on the Export of Live Animals. He said: Facilities at Holyhead are far and away better than anything else I have seen, either in the United Kingdom or on the continent. There is sufficient

lairage in one block to handle 1,500 cattle daily and this number was passing through the lairage almost every day up to 1969. The number was slashed as a result of the burning of the railway bridge across the Menai Straits. The lairage itself is connected to a quiet harbour and the boats dock at a point with connections to well-constructed passages leading into different pens. The unloading ramp is adjustable and the animals walk off the ship and are directed along the passages with high concrete walls and with ample room, and are diverted into their various lairages. As a member of the O'Brien Committee established by the British Government to investigate conditions affecting the export of live animals from Britain, I also feel that the excellent facilities at Holyhead coupled with the short sea journey and the close proximity of the North Wales fattening areas [...] enable cattle to be transported under exceptionally humane conditions and with the least possible discomfort to the beasts. In the light of debates we have had in this House, that is a very significant paragraph. I am surprised that this important factor should have been so lightly dismissed by British Railways.

My hon. Friend the Minister for Transport said in answer to my Question last week that he based his decision on the commercial judgment of British Railways. I do not share his confidence in that judgment. British Railways abandon their best cattle port—the best in Western Europe, according to Professor Williams—withdraw the service when the traffic is on the upturn, argue at the inquiry that there would be a decline in live cattle imports from Ireland, and adduce no evidence in support. The expert evidence is to the contrary.

It emerged that British Railways had lost interest in carrying cattle and had taken no positive action to reduce their operational costs and attract additional trade. What kind of commercial judgment is this supposed to be? It is a small, short-term saving in return for a long-term loss to the nation.

In response, the Minister of State, Department of the Environment, Denis Howell commented,

The decision by British Rail to close the cattle ferry was taken in the light of hard economic facts. For some years now the level of cattle traffic passing through Holyhead has declined significantly. In seven years the level dropped by almost a half. Compared with 143,000 head which passed through in 1967, only 73,000 were imported to Holyhead in 1974. Based on traffic in the first 10 months of this year, the effect of the decline was that the service was losing some £650,000 a year.

The closure, from Sunday, will have resulted in an immediate improvement in current cash flow for the Board of over £110,000 a year. These figures take no account of the £2 million or so new investment in capital equipment which would have been required in the next five years had the service been kept running. I am told that £1.8 million of that would have been for new cattle wagons and £0.2 million for improved dock facilities.

The *Slieve Donard*'s Holyhead career was a short one – just sixteen years. General cargo was now the preserve of the container ships *Brian Boroime* and *Rhodri Mawr*.

She had been a much-loved ship, despite her trade, and along with the older 'Slieves' was the first command of many Holyhead Masters coming up through the ranks. Captain Glynne Pritchard recalls life on the old cargo ships:

On each of the cargo ships there were usually four Master Mariners each with a Foreign-going Master's certificate. So all the officers had sailed deep sea previously. There were the Captain, Chief Officer and two 2nd Officers.

There were four Engineer Officers with the Chief usually in possession of a combined Steam and Motor certificate. The second and usually the third were certificated. Alongside in Holyhead and Dublin there would be a Deck Officer and an Engineer Officer on watch.

The ship sailed from Holyhead at 3.00 a.m. We would all join the ship in the evening in order to get some sleep before sailing.

Half an hour before sailing the 2nd Officer would proceed to the steering flat with the Chief Engineer. The junior 2nd Officer would be on the Bridge. On instructions from aft the wheel would be turned both ways and checked that all was in order. The junior 2nd would then check everything on the Bridge to ensure that all was in order; such things as navigation lights, signalling lamp, radar and Decca navigator. The Chief Officer would make rounds of the whole ship to see that all was in order.

Just before sailing the Captain and Chief Officer with the Quartermaster and lookout would be on the Bridge. Senior 2nd Officer, aft and Jr 2nd Officer for'd with the carpenter and crew. We would single up fore and aft to a headrope and sternrope and two back springs. Ship's papers detailing the cargo on board would then be sent to the ship. Permission from the Boathouse would then be obtained by radio to sail and we would be on our way. We would also radio a shore station to give them our name and where sailing to.

When clear of the harbour, the two 2nd Officers would come on the bridge and we would all stay there until the South Stack light was abeam, with the exception of the Chief Officer who would again make his rounds of the ship, when the Captain would 'set watches'. One of the three officers would take over the watch with a lookout and the others would go below. This officer would con the ship until half way across the Irish Sea when he would be relieved by one of the other officers. The officer who was not required to keep a watch was called 'the farmer'.

The Captain and officers would all be on the Bridge at the Kish Light and go on stations fore and aft when entering the Liffey. The Master would swing the ship in the Liffey and we would proceed astern to our berth at North Wall, where we would arrive before 8.00 a.m.

Cargo would be discharged and cattle would be loaded until ready for sailing around 8.00 p.m. In Dublin there would be one officer on watch and the others had various duties such as checking fire and life-saving appliances. Once a week there would be fire and emergency stations and boat drill.

The *Hibernia* alongside the station, Holyhead. (David Jones)

The *Holyhead Ferry I* under construction at Hawthorn Leslie at Hebburn on Tyne. (Nigel Thornton Collection)

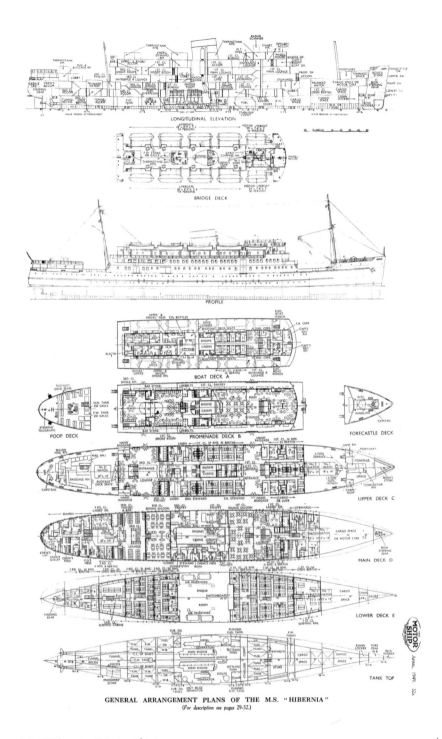

GENERAL ARRANGEMENT PLANS OF THE M.S. "HIBERNIA"
(For description see pages 29-32.)

Plans of the *Hibernia*. (*Motor Ship*)

The *Holyhead Ferry I* leaves Dun Laoghaire's East Pier. (Ian Collard)

An evening view of the *Holyhead Ferry 1* at Salt Island. (David Jones)

A view from the bridge of the *Holyhead Ferry I* at sea. (Captain Walter Lloyd Williams)

The smoke room on the *Holyhead Ferry I*. (Nigel Thornton Collection)

The *Holyhead Ferry I* loading at the East Pier, Dun Laoghaire. (Jim Ashby)

The *Holyhead Ferry 1* picks her way through yachts outside Dun Laoghaire Harbour. (Jim Ashby)

The cargo vessel *Slieve Bawn*. (Captain Glynne Pritchard Collection)

The cattle run at Holyhead. (Justin Merrigan Collection)

Holyhead Goods Shed. (Justin Merrigan Collection)

Holyhead Station, awning and hotel. (Justin Merrigan Collection)

Above: The car ferry *Dover* at Holyhead. (Ian Collard)

Below left: The *Caledonian Princess* berthed at Salt Island, Holyhead. (David Jones)

Below right: An aerial view of *Holyhead Ferry I.* (Justin Merrigan Collection)

St Michael's Pier at
Dun Laoghaire under
construction. (Captain
Simon Coate Collection)

Opening of St Michael's
Pier at Dun Laoghaire
in 1969. (Captain Simon
Coate Collection)

Cars disembark from the
Holyhead Ferry 1 at Dun
Laoghaire. (Jim Ashby)

The cargo vessel *Harrogate* loading at Dublin. (Ian Collard)

The *Slieve Donard* at Holyhead. (Captain Walter Lloyd Williams)

Holyhead harbour with the *Cambria* at the station berth. (Ian Collard)

The *Hibernia* dressed overall, along with the *Slieve League*, on the occasion of a royal visit to Holyhead. (Justin Merrigan Collection)

The *Selby* at Heysham. (Jim Ashby)

The *Cambria* leaving Holyhead on the occasion of a royal visit. (Captain Walter Lloyd Williams)

The *Cambria* at Dun Laoghaire. (Captain Walter Lloyd Williams)

The *Cambria* and the *Container Venturer* at Heysham. (Captain Walter Lloyd Williams)

The *Cambria* at Heysham. (Captain Walter Lloyd Williams)

The Transporter Crane at Holyhead under construction. (Justin Merrigan Collection)

The *Slieve Bawn* alongside Gotto Wharf at Belfast as demolition gets underway to make way for the new container terminal. (Captain Walter Lloyd Williams)

The cargo vessel *Colchester*. (Jim Ashby)

The *Isle of Ely* at Dublin. (Jim Ashby)

The *Holyhead Ferry I.* (Captain Walter Lloyd Williams)

The *Cambria* leaving Holyhead. (Captain Walter Lloyd Williams)

Revised brochure, Holyhead–Dun Laoghaire from 1 August 1971. (Ian Collard Collection)

The container vessels *Rhodri Mawr* and *Brian Boroime* at Holyhead. (Chris Howell)

The dredger *Pick Me Up*. (John Hodgkinson Collection)

The *Pick Me Up* at work in Holyhead. (John Hodgkinson Collection)

The *Pick Me Up* in dry dock at Holyhead. (Captain Glynne Pritchard Collection)

Crew of the dredger *Pick Me Up*.
(John Hodgkinson Collection)

Berths 8, 9 and 10 at Holyhead.
(Justin Merrigan Collection)

The *Maid of Kent* leaves
Holyhead after a dry-docking
in 1969. (Captain Walter Lloyd
Williams)

Pelham Gate, Marine Yard at Holyhead. (Justin Merrigan Collection)

Loading mail on board the *Cambria* at Holyhead. (Captain George Davey Collection)

The *Holyhead Ferry I* sailing from Dun Laoghaire. (Captain Walter Lloyd Williams)

British Rail Car Ferries brochure featuring the *Dover*. (Captain George Davey Collection)

Captain George Davey on the bridge of the *Cambria* at Dun Laoghaire in 1973.

The *Hibernia* at Dun Laoghaire. (Ian Collard)

7

End of the Mail Service

In March 1975, a £16 million order for a large new ship was placed with Aalborg Vaerft A/S of Aalborg, Denmark. Specially designed for service to Dun Laoghaire, the new ship would replace the *Cambria* and the *Hibernia*, as well as the *Holyhead Ferry I*. What followed this news was two years of chopping and changing as a variety of ships came and went. On 3 March, the *Holyhead Ferry I* launched the new year-round ro-ro service for commercial vehicles. Operating daily, except Sundays, the new order with the car ferry was one round trip per day, with extra sailings between 2 July and 4 October. She was quickly swapped with the *Dover* due to the English Channel ship's capacity for 205 cars compared with her half-sister's 153 cars. To enable the new service to become operational, the old import shed in the inner harbour was converted into a temporary customs clearance point until more permanent facilities were provided at Salt Island and a new vehicle ramp completed on the departures berth at the station.

Then came the *Duke of Argyll*, spending her final summer as a British Rail ship, surplus to requirements since the closure of her Heysham–Belfast service. As reserve ship at Holyhead she lasted until September when she sailed to Barrow for layup, pending sale. Meanwhile, her sister, the *Duke of Rothesay*, maintained services alongside the *Dover* until she was replaced by the *Duke of Lancaster* in July, herself having been released at Fishguard by the newly converted *Avalon*. The end of the time-honoured mail service also came in 1975 and it fell to the *Cambria* to take the last such sailing from Dun Laoghaire on Sunday 7 September. Under the command of Captain Ivor Griffiths, she slipped out of Holyhead for the final time at 11.00 p.m. on 28 October 1975. She arrived at Barrow at 9.00 a.m. the following morning and remained there until sold to Orri Navigation of Saudi Arabia in January 1976. Renamed *Al Taif* she sank while at anchor in Suez Roads in January 1981.

The *Avalon*, British Rail's largest Irish Sea ship, arrived for her first spell at Holyhead beginning on 11 January 1976. Her time on the run was marred by an unfortunate incident on 17 March. Arriving at Holyhead in dense fog with the 2045 sailing from Dun Laoghaire, she made contact with the T-Piece on the Mail Pier, damaging some 20 feet of starboard-side plating. The service was subsequently suspended for three days, unheard of in the days of the mail ships, while replacement tonnage was sourced. It was a complex affair, involving the movement of the *Maid of Kent* from Weymouth to Fishguard and the *Dover* moving from Fishguard to Holyhead where she took up service at 3.45 p.m. on 20 March. After her repairs, the *Avalon* was back on the run on 10 April, operating alongside the *Hibernia*, and remained there until relieved by the *Dover* allowing her to return to Fishguard on 25 June. The *Hibernia* remained on the Holyhead link until Sunday 3 October 1976, when she arrived at Holyhead with her final sailing from Dun Laoghaire. After sale to Agapitos Brothers of Greece, she was renamed *Express Apollon*. On 18 December 1980, the old ship was observed at Bombay and four weeks later she was at Darukhana in India, where Solid Steel Traders began demolition.

Taking up service the day after the *Hibernia*'s withdrawal was the *Avalon* again, swapping with the *Dover*, which in turn moved to Fishguard. Once again, she was to blot her copybook and, on 17 October, she failed with generator problems while alongside at Dun Laoghaire. Services were again cancelled until, in a repeat move, the *Maid of Kent* was called to Fishguard from Weymouth to release the *Dover*, which sailed north to restore Holyhead services.

In 1976, Captain John Rowlands retired as Master of the *Holyhead Ferry 1*. During his time with British Rail at Holyhead, he had entertained many important guests sailing to and from Ireland including such well-known names as Jayne Mansfield, Alma Cogan and the trumpeter Eddie Calvert. Joining the Holyhead Railway steamers in 1946 after service with Ellerman's as Chief Officer, John found himself working his way up from the bottom again! He sailed on all the ships at that time including the *Slieve Bloom*, *Slieve Donard*, *Slieve League* and the *Slieve More*, the *Princess Maud* and many other passenger steamers. Eventually, he was promoted to Chief Officer on the *Hibernia* and a few years later as Master of the *Cambria*. With the rationalisation of services, Captain Rowlands was not alone in retiring. Captain Ivor Griffiths, Senior Master at the port, also stood down after a long and distinguished career and so too did Captain George Davey and Captain Alex Roberston, both taking advantage of early retirement. Gaining his first command in 1962, on the *Slieve Bloom*, Captain Davey recalls being in charge of the ship on leaving Holyhead, when she inexplicably stopped responding to the helm. He managed to take the ship out of the harbour under the engines alone. The ship was anchored in the outer harbour to investigate. It became apparent that the rudder had fallen off, probably as a result of metal fatigue in the shaft! The missing rudder was recovered some years later during dredging operations in the harbour and can now be seen at Holyhead's Maritime Museum.

As for the *Holyhead Ferry I*, now an official Dover ship, she was sent to Swan Hunter on the Tyne for conversion to drive-through operation from which she emerged in September 1976, renamed *Earl Leofric*. The *Caledonian Princess* was back in service at Holyhead in December, replacing the *Dover* and operating alongside the *Duke of Lancaster*. This was the final time the former Stranraer ship served on the Dun Laoghaire run, standing down on the last day of February 1977. In her place came the *Avalon*, pending delivery of the new *St Columba* from Denmark. The 'Caley P' then sailed south to the English Channel where she saw out her British Rail career, becoming Dover's last steamer in the process. Aalborg Vaerft didn't waste any time with construction on the new Holyhead ship and, in July 1976, yard number 214 was ready to take to the water for the first time. But as so often happens in these cases, the weather had different plans! Thursday 15 July saw a chartered Aer Lingus 737 fly from Dublin, via Heathrow, with a representative group of British and Irish guests to witness the launch of the new ship. The following day saw high winds, the direction of which caused the level of water in Lim Fjord, on which Aalborg stands, to drop. With the water level just four inches too low to safely take the ship, the invited guests had to settle for the naming ceremony, which went ahead with Mrs Joan Kirby, wife of British Rail's Shipping and International Services Division's general manager David Kirby, performing the honours. With suitable tidal conditions the *St Columba* finally took to the water on Saturday 17 July with Mrs Kirby launching the vessel, unfortunately, after the departure of the guests for London and Dublin on their pre-arranged charter flight.

Sea trials for the *St Columba* were carried out in the Kattegat over the weekend of 18 March 1977, and at 5.00 a.m. on Saturday 2 April, she sailed from Aalborg for Holyhead under the command of Captain Len Evans. On the following day the *St Columba* arrived at Dover's Western Docks where minor engine adjustments were carried out. The next morning, she was on her way again and at 2.00 p.m. on Tuesday 5 April she arrived at her new home port to be given a rapturous welcome by more than 5,000 people crowding every vantage point to see the new ship.

Speaking of the *St Columba*'s performance on passage to Holyhead, Captain Evans said,

> Although the weather conditions on the delivery voyage did not exceed Force 7, the ship behaved admirably, and her sea-keeping qualities lived up to our best expectations. This was of course further confirmed after she went into service and during subsequent winters.

The new ship dominated the scene at Holyhead. She was a much-needed breath of fresh air to the service, which, since the withdrawal of the *Hibernia* and the *Cambria*, was operated by a variety of stop-gap, steam turbine car ferries. On Tuesday 19 April, the *St Columba* had a trial run around Holyhead Bay and, on Sunday 24 April, she was open to the public at Holyhead, an event that attracted 1,704 visitors. This was a time of celebration for all connected with the link and, on Wednesday 27 April, the *St Columba* undertook her inaugural voyage to Dun Laoghaire with members of the Irish Government, British Rail Board, tour operators, journalists and other VIPs on board. There were two sets of officers on board: Captain Len Evans and Captain John Peters as masters, the latter taking her out of Holyhead, Walter Lloyd Williams and Lewis Pritchard as Chief Officers, Trevor Salmon and Dai Davies as 2nd Officers, and Tudor Jones and Glynne Pritchard as 3rd Officers. That evening, guests attended a dinner at the Royal Marine Hotel, addressed by An Taoiseach (Irish Premier) Mr Liam Cosgrave, TD. The Chairman of British Rail, Mr Peter Parker, offered a toast to the new ship:

> The *St Columba* as a symbol of strengthened ties between the people of Ireland, the people of Britain and the people of Europe.

Taking up commercial service on Monday 2 May, the *St Columba* was an overnight success on the route. With a capacity for 2,400 passengers, 335 cars or 36 trucks (or a mixture of the two), nothing quite like the ship had ever seen before on the Irish Sea. Little wonder was it that after just over one year in operation the *St Columba* had carried her millionth passenger. As built, the *St Columba*'s passenger accommodation was spread between first and second class. The entrance areas and circulation halls for both classes featured single staircases varying in width from 6.5 to 9 metres which, from A Deck, led up to the Boat Deck and down to B Deck. The staircases, with open risers in the flights upwards from A, were sited centrally in the halls. The first class areas were carpeted, the second class having PVC floor covering. The finishes and decorative schemes were identical in both classes. Perimeter bulkheads were boldly patterned in brown and black; the slatted ceilings were orange. A cream freize between the two and the bright metal of the ballustrades enlivened these unusually low-key colour combinations. The ancillary services around the staircase halls included a Bureau and 'Sealink Shop' for each class.

On A Deck aft, a Tea Bar decorated in greens, greys and white accommodated 196 diners with self-service catering facilities. Beyond this, at the aft extreme of the accommodation, were enclosed shelter spaces with provision for 234 travellers. Port and starboard the seats were arranged for viewing out to sea and a disco with small dance floor was also provided. Further enclosed shelter accommodation was provided on the Boat Deck where a TV Lounge seating fifty was flanked port, starboard and aft by a further 224 seats. The shelter accommodation on both decks featured continuous runs of large viewing windows. The vertical steel of the hull was exposed and white painted at the ship's side. Cream slatted ceilings and brown or grey deck coverings provided the seating for brightly coloured seats, tables and interior bulkheads.

The Lansdowne Road Bar (second class) aft on B Deck seated 122 passengers centrally and ninety-two in each of the linked port and starboard lounges. While it was very different in character from the Cardiff Arms Park Bar for first class passengers, the Lansdowne Road Bar shared a similar use of brown, cream and orange colours. First Class accommodation with seating for 544 passengers (excluding the restaurant) was located forward on A and B Decks. Whereas the Lansdowne Road Bar was predominantly orange in colour, the Cardiff Arms Park Bar, forward of the staircase on B Deck, used orange in only small areas of ceiling and bar service area and in the central seating. The bulkheads were brown and black, similar to the adjacent entrance but in a much smaller pattern. Perimeter seating was black. Each pair of these seats and the bulkhead behind were curved to respond to an adjacent circular table. Above these groupings illuminated orange circular coffers were set in a brown background. The central ceiling area was white. The Cardiff Arms Park Bar was an entirely interior space without windows. However, it did link directly with a small lounge, seating twenty-four passengers, where the soft lighting and restrained colour changed sharply to a contrastingly bright orange, white and purple enclosure.

Port and starboard of the Cardiff Arms Park Bar were two lounges, each capable of seating seventy-eight passengers in spaces where browns derived from the adjacent areas were complemented by seats and bulkheads in different shades of lilac. First class accommodation on A Deck comprised three lounges and the restaurant, the latter being situated aft of the staircase. The restaurant was decorated in shades of red and claret and extended the full width of the ship. It was also capable of being subdivided into a central area seating forty-eight with port and starboard spaces each seating twenty diners.

Forward of the staircase there were two small side spaces, both approached through a central lounge. The portside lounge in shades of tan and yellow seated sixty-six passengers while a TV Lounge on the starboard side could accommodate forty-eight passengers in a predominantly blue space. This latter lounge was probably co-author Justin Merrigan's favourite lounge in the entire ship, and he can still recall passing many crossings in cosy comfort there!

The central lounge itself could seat ninety-four passengers in settees, armchairs and bulkhead seats of which the backs extended virtually to the ceiling. The very simple decorative scheme in greens and cream was dominated by a three-dimensional, glass-fibre mural the full height of the room by some 5.5 m in width. Executed by the late Franta Belsky, it illustrated aspects of the life of St Columba. The mural extended between the two entrance doors on the aft bulkhead of the area. Its intrinsic interest was enhanced by the presence in the room of the sculptor's first 1:10 scale model for the work which was acquired and presented to the ship by her sponsor, Mrs David Kirby. The fitting-out of all public spaces on *St Columba* was carried out by Aalborg Vaerft A/S to the designs of architects Ward Associates of London.

The ship was reduced to stern-loading operation when, on 9 December, a mobile crane collapsed across the Carlisle Pier vehicle ramp at Dun Laoghaire. Until the ramp could be repaired, the ship operated for several days arriving at her usual rail-connected berth to discharge foot passengers before then moving across to St Michael's Pier where she berthed stern-in to discharge and load vehicles.

The former *Holyhead Ferry I* saw one final stint of Irish Sea service before sale to Spanish breakers in 1981 when, in January 1978, she returned to the route for which she was built, on relief duties during the *St Columba*'s first overhaul. The *Earl Leofric* was not blessed with good weather for her return and, on 28 January, she took ten hours to cross to Dun Laoghaire in storm-force conditions. On 21 February, she contacted with the ramp at Dun Laoghaire's St Michael's Pier causing damage to her bow visor and reducing her to stern loading for the remainder of her stay. That a ship should be scrapped after just sixteen years in service may be absurd, but thirsty steam turbines and a woefully inadequate vehicle-deck design had no place in the modern age of double-decked motor ships. Ironically, her replacement at Dover in October 1980, the new *St Anselm*, was transferred to Holyhead in 1991 and renamed *Stena Cambria*.

As traffic continued to grow, British Rail further strengthened the Dun Laoghaire service in 1978 by introducing the ro-ro vessel *Dalriada* alongside the *St Columba* and the *Duke of Lancaster* for the summer season, primarily to release space on the larger ship's vehicle deck for cars. Before she could arrive to take up her slot the company chartered in near-sister *Transbaltica* from June until the *Dalriada* made her debut in August.

Sealink UK Ltd

British Rail ownership of shipping services continued through the 1970s. On 1 January 1979 the Shipping and International Services Division ceased to exist and its function, assets and staff were transferred to a new company wholly owned by the Board and titled Sealink UK Ltd. The trade name of Sealink had been used for British Railways' marine services, along with the shipping services of the continental railways organisations since January 1970.

Having already seen the freight vessel *Anderida* in service to Dun Laoghaire alongside the *Avalon* during the *St Columba*'s overhaul period, the chartered ro-ro *Stena Timer* took up service on 24 May 1979 in a repeat of the freight service offered by the *Dalriada* in 1978. There had been hopes that the ship might be retained beyond September on a year-round basis; however, issues with manning levels brought her withdrawal as planned.

Probably one of the most unusual ferries to operate out of Holyhead was the Harwich train ferry *Cambridge Ferry*, appearing on 28 May 1980, seven days after the Dun Laoghaire route was plunged into chaos when the *St Columba* broke down on passage. The car ferry's place was taken by the *Avalon* on 22 May but she too was to fail, with boiler trouble, after one week on the 'Columba's' roster. Things were kept moving through the introduction of the Heysham ro-ro *Lagan Bridge* on 23 May, but passenger traffic was diverted to Liverpool and Fishguard. While all this was going on, the train ferry was in Holyhead's dry dock and so the decision was taken to press her into service for a couple of days on completion of her overall. A level of normality returned on 30 May when Stranraer's *Ailsa Princess* arrived to maintain passenger services until the return of the *Avalon* on 2 June. It was 12 June before the *St Columba* returned.

Another Stranraer ship appeared in the camp in the form of the *Antrim Princess*. She took up the Dun Laoghaire route with the afternoon sailing on 17 January 1981, relieving the *St Columba*, which sailed to Avonmouth for refit. Standing down on 11 February and sailing to Belfast that same day, this was the *Antrim Princess*'s second visit to the Holyhead–Dun Laoghaire route, the first being in 1973 when she stood in for one sailing on 15 December.

One of the more unusual Sealink vessels to visit Holyhead was the Harwich-based grab-dredger *Landguard*. Built in 1960 for the British Transport Commission by Goole Shipbuilding & Repairing Co. Ltd, the *Landguard* spent almost her entire career on the River Stour, but in Sealink years was to travel as far as Stranraer and Holyhead for dredging operations at her owner's ports. On one passage to Holyhead, the main engine-cooling water pipe ruptured causing flooding in the bilges and forcing the vessel to stop some twenty-eight miles from Portland Bill. With water rising rapidly, repairs were made by passing a bandage around the fractured pipe and the vessel was able to make for Weymouth for a more permanent fix. On another occasion, on passage in the Irish Sea in Force 12 conditions, a passing ship called up to advise he had just seen daylight between the *Landguard*'s keel and the top of the waves!

Each summer, a second ship was deployed at Holyhead to augment the *St Columba*'s sailings to Dun Laoghaire. Such notable steamers as the *Duke of Lancaster*, *Lord*

Warden and *Avalon* all partnered the crack ship, the latter regularly switching between Fishguard and Holyhead as overhaul and emergency relief until 1979, when she was replaced at the Pembrokeshire port by the *Stena Normandica*. On 8 September 1980, the *Avalon* left Dun Laoghaire on her final commercial sailing under the Sealink flag. She sailed to Barrow on 24 September for lay-up pending sale and three months later, with funnel painted black and the first letter of her name removed, she sailed to Pakistan. Despite being just seventeen years old, her thirsty turbines made her unattractive to any interested buyers and she arrived at Gadani Beach, on 22 January 1981. H.H. Steel Ltd commenced breaking immediately.

Allocated to Holyhead in the *Avalon*'s place was the last of four new ships from Harland & Wolff, the *St David*. However, by the time the *Avalon* had been disposed of it was obvious that the newbuild would be so late that she would miss the bulk of the 1981 summer season. To fill the gap Holyhead's management were keen to have Dover's *Hengist*, but this was rejected and instead an old friend came steaming north. Like the *Holyhead Ferry 1*, the *Dover* also underwent major surgery from which she emerged in 1977 as a drive-through ship renamed the *Earl Siward*. As such she was to enjoy one final spell of service at Holyhead operating the additional 'second ship' summer sailings from 22 June 1981. She served for just seventeen days before being replaced by the chartered *Prinsessan Desirée*. When the *Earl Siward* quietly departed Dun Laoghaire under a cloud of black smoke on 8 July, the few onlookers on the piers were not just witnessing the ship's final departure, but the end of an era as the last railway-owned turbine steamer to operate on the Irish Sea disappeared over the horizon. The ship was sold four months later, moving to Cyprus as the *Sol Express*. In 1993, she returned to the UK having been purchased for use as a night club on the Tyne at Gateshead by Absolute Leisure, the operators of the *Tuxedo Princess*, another former British Rail ferry – the *Caledonian Princess*. As the *Tuxedo Royale*, she traded there for six years before being replaced by the *Tuxedo Princess* on her return from a failed venture in Glasgow. The *Tuxedo Royale* was then moved south to Middlesbrough for similar operation. But this too, somewhat predictably, was set to end in failure. The sale of the *Tuxedo Princess* to Turkish shipbreakers seemed set to confirm the 'Royale's' future, but in 2010 she remained laid up, slowly rusting away at Able Central Quay at Middlesbrough, just below the Transporter Bridge.

Replacing the *Earl Siward*, the chartered, 1971-built *Prinsessan Desirée* entered service to Dun Laoghaire on 9 July 1981. The ship had just completed a stint with B&I Line on the Rosslare–Pembroke service when the Irish company sub-chartered her to Sealink pending delivery of the *St David* from builders Harland & Wolff. Her time on the service was plagued by bad press; passengers found her rather dated Scandinavian interior to be less than comfortable. The arrival into service of the *St David* on 10 August 1981 saw the Swedish ship return to more familiar waters in Gothenburg.

Holyhead's Marine Superintendent, Captain Hubert Hughes, retired in 1981. A Holyhead man, Hubert Hughes first went to sea at the age of fifteen and served four years as a cadet officer with P. Henderson & Co., Glasgow, before taking his Second Mate's certificate in 1942. He was appointed 3rd Officer on the *Hensada*. After gaining his 1st Officer's ticket, he joined Ellerman Line where he got his Master's ticket. He then joined the LMS ships at Holyhead, initially sailing on the *Slieve Bloom* and all railway vessels at the port before being appointed as Holyhead's Marine Superintendent after command of the cargo vessel *Harrogate*. Captain Hughes worked closely with Captain Len Evans, both ensuring the successful entry into service of the new *St Columba* in 1977.

As we have already seen, the *St Columba* was a fine sea ship, but the Irish Sea can be an unkind place. Saturday 19 December 1981 saw the Irish Sea at its worst, this being the night the Penlee Lifeboat RNLB *Solomon Browne* was lost with her entire crew going to the aid of the coaster *Union Star* in the western English Channel. For Captain Len Evans, Chief Officer Glynne Pritchard and 2nd officers David Farrell and Ken Jones on the *St Columba* it was a long first passage in their twenty-four hours on duty. With winds at Force 12-plus, the ship was hove to off the Kish Tower for eight hours, conditions at Dun Laoghaire being impossible to even consider an attempt at berthing. She eventually got alongside at Dun Laoghaire at 6.30 a.m. the following morning, fourteen hours after leaving Holyhead.

In December 1982, Captain Evans, unable to berth at Dun Laoghaire due to a south-east gale Force 11-12, sailed slowly south from the Kish Lighthouse.

In the vicinity of the Codling I found myself looking up at the sea from the bridge! Needless to say I did not stay down there for long, and was most surprised when a German ship called me up asking if I could assist him, because he, as the giving way vessel, was concerned not to alter course because his cargo of phosphates could ship. One touch on the *St Columba*'s telegraphs and she was away like a scalded cat, much to the admiration and relief of the German.

Arriving at Dun Laoghaire in an easterly gale was not always easy. Captain John Bakewell recalls:

I used to come well up to the east and then swing towards the west so that the ship was lying at right angles to Carlisle Pier. We would slowly work her in so that the port side aft was alongside the knuckle. Two stern lines would be run out and when fast and tight, the bow thrust was used to push the bow to port. This worked nearly every time. If it didn't work the beauty was that you could abort the manoeuvre and steam out.

Meanwhile, history was made in March 1982 when Ireland's B&I Line commenced their car ferry service from Dublin, bringing competition to Sealink's doorstep. The news was greeted with howls of protest in the Welsh port. With the Marine Workshops already under threat, Sealink workers, fearful for their future livelihoods, protested by blockading the entrance to Holyhead Harbour thereby preventing the Irish ship access for berthing trials. The repeated failure of their ships to berth at Holyhead led B&I crews to take retaliatory action. While the *Connacht* was returning to Dublin having failed to berth at Holyhead a crew boarded the laid-up *Munster* in Dublin and sailed her across the bay to Dun Laoghaire where she dropped anchor in the mouth of the harbour. Her intentions: to prevent access to any Sealink vessel.

With a one-hour-and-thirty-minutes head start over the returning *Connacht*, the *St David* approached Dublin Bay at 6.00 p.m. to find her way into the harbour well and truly blocked. On the bridge of the approaching *St David*, Captain Idwal Pritchard and his officers looked at ways of getting their ship into Dun Laoghaire. Calling the *Munster* by VHF radio to ask of their intentions Captain Pritchard was initially met with silence but the Irish ship eventually indicated they would not be moving. Asking if the Munster was anchored the *St David* was given a blunt 'yes'. Then followed the first of several attempts to break the blockade. The *St David* went for a gap between the *Munster*'s bow and the East Pier lighthouse, prompting a warning from the *Munster*'s Master that small boats were placed between his ship and the wall. The *St David* moved astern and coming to rest about a ship's length from the anchored vessel. She then made another run for a gap between the *Munster*'s stern and the West Pier but using her engines, the B&I ship moved to block the ship again. Still the *St David* continued her approach, finally coming to a halt seemingly within a few feet of the *Munster*. The Irish ship was completely dwarfed but nonetheless unperturbed by the 'David'. After a few breathtaking moments the *St David* again moved astern.

From ashore there was no doubt; the *Munster* had placed himself and the *St David* in a highly dangerous situation. Captain Pritchard had full command of his highly manoeuvrable and was able to do exactly what he wanted with her. This game of cat and mouse continued for well over an hour but each time the *Munster* thwarted the British ship's attempts. Finally, shortly before midnight the *St David* returned to Holyhead for stores and a reappraisal of the situation. The following morning, with Captain Pritchard once again on the bridge, the *St David* reappeared off Dun Laoghaire again finding the *Munster* firmly blockading the harbour entrance. However, by now the Sealink ferry had an unwell passenger on board and following a doctor's call for urgent medical treatment the *Munster* moved aside on humanitarian grounds. Sailing through the harbour entrance at a rate of knots the *St David* quickly proceeded to her Carlisle Pier Berth. After a very quick turnaround the *St David* sailed again for Holyhead and with all sailings suspended until further notice the B&I ship returned to her berth in Dublin.

On 7 April, B&I's *Leinster* finally entered Holyhead unopposed. Reinstated members of the National Union of Railwaymen who had previously been dismissed for refusing to work B&I ships handled her at the Station Berth. With the Welsh Dragon and the Red Ensign flying from her mast, the *Leinster* occupied the berth vacated thirty minutes earlier by the *St Columba*. Holyhead's link with Ireland was reopened after one long month without sailings. By 1987 the Irish company had closed their 153-year-old Liverpool service in order to concentrate on the shorter, and more economical, Holyhead crossing.

The *St David*'s Senior Master, Captain Idwal Pritchard, retired in 1982. His father was Chief Officer of the *Scotia* at Dunkirk. He served on deck with Blue Funnel and sat the examination for 2nd Officer whilst ashore recuperating from an accident he suffered on the *Talthybius*. He then joined Lamport & Holt's for a short while, later transferring to Clan Line, with whom he obtained his Master FG certificate. Following in family tradition he joined British Railways at Holyhead in 1952. A co-founder and

Chairman of the then-new Holyhead Maritime Museum, Idwal's younger brother Glynne was also a Holyhead Master.

Winter 1982 saw the conversion of the *St Columba* from a two-class ship to a one-class and what was to be the first of a number of alterations to her comfortable accommodation. Sailing to Holyhead on 21 October was the *Ailsa Princess*, joining the *St David* over the Irish holiday weekend in the larger ship's absence. No sooner had this duty been completed than the *St David* broke down forcing a recall to service for the Weymouth-based ship. The *St Columba* returned to service in time for the Christmas rush complete with a large duty-free supermarket where the second class tea bar had been situated and with all former second class areas carpeted. Unfortunately, she came to grief while berthing at Dun Laoghaire in storm conditions, forcing her to run as a stern loader until visor repairs could be completed after the peak.

Engine trouble was to strike the *St Columba* again on 4 August 1983, but this time at the height of the summer season, causing maximum disruption. Operating on her starboard engine and with a crossing time of over five hours, the *St Columba* struggled on alongside a constantly full *St David* until a replacement could be brought in. A Holyhead crew was dispatched to Calais to collect the French-flagged *Villandry* on charter from Sealink partners SNCF and arriving in the Welsh port on 7 August, the ship took up the run two days later after a major cleaning-up operation – she had been laid up on a coal berth! Captain John Bakewell was at first appointed Staff Captain with a very pleasant Breton as Captain. Captain Bakewell recalls,

> He asked me if we could swap jobs as he was unfamiliar with the Irish Sea. This was agreed so he went as Staff Captain with me in command of a ship flying the French Tricolor!

Meanwhile, as the disruption made Irish national headlines, Holyhead's engineers excelled themselves working to return the *St Columba* to service as quickly as possible. Returning to service on 11 August, the relief at having her back was short-lived for, on the following morning, the opposite Stork Werkspoor TM410 engine failed. The *Villandry* was hastily called back and she operated for a further three days while the 'Columba' was dealt with.

The *Hibernia* at Dun
Laoghaire in 1974.
(Dermot Bremner)

The *Cambria's* last
sailing, 7 September
1975. (Captain Glynne
Pritchard)

The *Duke of Lancaster*
and the *Dover*. (Justin
Merrigan Collection)

The *St Columba* on the slipway prior to her launch at Aalborg, Denmark. (Jim Ashby)

The *Duke of Rothesay* 'makes smoke' departing Dun Laoghaire. (Don Smith – Pictureships)

The *St Columba* at the refit berth at Holyhead just prior to entering service. (John Marsh)

An Taoiseach Mr Liam Cosgrave and BR Ireland Manager Clement Preece with Captain Len Evans on the occasion of the *St Columba*'s inaugural sailing from Dun Laoghaire, 28 April 1977.

The *St Columba* sails from her Inner Harbour berth at Holyhead. (Ian Scott Taylor)

The *Duke of Lancaster*, inward from Dun Laoghaire passes the outbound *St Columba* at Holyhead. (Chris Howell)

The *St Columba* sails
with a good load of
passengers. (Chris
Howell)

The *Duke of
Lancaster* arriving
at Holyhead. (Kenny
Whyte)

The *Duke of Lancaster*
alongside the Admiralty
Pier between sailings.
(Stephen Poultain)

Right: A pre-sailing deck scene on board the *Duke of Lancaster* at Holyhead as Chief Officer Tudor Jones makes his way to the aft bridge for departure. (Kenny Whyte)

Below: The *St Columba*, *Dalriada* and the *Duke of Lancaster* at Dun Laoghaire in 1978. (Kenny Whyte)

The *St Columba* leaving Glasgow on 1 April 1979. The ship sailed out of the basin using her after bridge and bow rudder. The Clyde Pilot was impressed and, as there was a very strong breeze, he advised the Holyhead master, Captain Len Evans, to 'keep going'! And keep going she did, seventeen miles stern first before swinging at Greenock and proceeding ahead. (Kenny Whyte)

The *Lord Warden* arriving at Holyhead in 1979, her Red Ensign at half mast, probably in August, in respect for Lord Mountbatten, who was assassinated in that month. (Kenny Whyte)

Weymouth's *Maid of Kent* arrives at Dun Laoghaire on relief duties. (Jack Phelan)

With a busy port in the background, a Class 40-40055 prepares to leave Holyhead in 1979. (Chris Howell)

The classic steamer *Caesarea* in 1980, a visitor to Holyhead's dry dock prior to her final season on the Dover Strait. (Kenny Whyte)

With an aft line to help her pull off the station berth, the *Avalon* moves into position before letting go and moving astern through the Inner Harbour at Holyhead. (Kenny Whyte)

An *Avalon* passenger's view of the fo'c'sle on departure from Holyhead. 2nd Officer Richard Jones (left) and Carpenter Ken Robertson. (Kenny Whyte)

A view from the bridge of the *Avalon* in the Irish Sea. (Kenny Whyte)

The *Express Apollon* (ex-*Hibernia)* laid up in Greece. (W. Owen Williams)

The *Express Apollon* (ex-*Hibernia*) at Kynnasora. (Albert Novelli)

Looking aft from the *Earl Leofric*'s monkey island. (Kenny Whyte)

The *St Columba* passes the *Earl Siward* at Holyhead. (Johan Inpijn)

The *Prinsessan Desirée* arrives at Dun Laoghaire, August 1981. (Justin Merrigan)

The *St David*. (Ken Larwood)

The *St David* slips
out of Holyhead past
a blockade of small
boats, to a retaliatory
blockade of Dun
Laoghaire Harbour
by B&I Line's
Munster. (Tony Jones)

B&I Line's *Munster*
blocks *St David*,
March 1982. (Justin
Merrigan Collection)

A pristine-looking
Ailsa Princess. (Don
Smith – Pictureships)

Holyhead's Station Clock in pieces next to the dry dock, now happily restored. (John Marsh)

Mate and Master brothers on the *St Columba*, Glynne and Idwal Pritchard.

The dredger *Landguard* berthed at Holyhead. (Justin Merrigan)

Above: A picture full of interest as the *St Columba* disembarks passengers at Dun Laoghaire. The rail-connected sailing sees the awaiting train ready to depart for Dublin, while Connaughton's chandlers wait for an empty car deck before storing the ship for her return sailing. (Jonathan Allen)

Right: Captain Walter Lloyd Williams on the aft bridge of the *St David*. (Captain Neville Lester)

8

Privatisation

Sealink UK Ltd was privatised in July 1984. In what was described as the 'Sale of the Century' the company, comprising thirty-seven ships, ten harbours and twenty-four routes, was sold to US-based Sea Containers for just £66 million. Major, and much-needed, investment was promised by company president Mr James B. Sherwood and, for Holyhead, larger ferries were promised, while the *St David* was transferred to Dover. In the meantime, in February 1985, the new Sealink British Ferries entered into an agreement with rivals B&I Line to rationalise sailings on the Irish Sea. The agreement provided for co-operation between the two companies and the elimination of sailing duplication on the Holyhead and Fishguard routes to Ireland. Outwardly, this brought to an end the tradition of a second summer ship for Sealink at Holyhead, the extra sailings being covered by B&I. While the *St David* had already been transferred to the England Channel, it had been planned to use the chartered Belgian ferry *Prins Phillippe* in her place at Holyhead, but this was now shelved. During overhaul periods, arrangements were put in place for B&I to deputise while the Sealink ships were in dry dock. By and large the move was not a popular one, especially with crews. The January 1986 overhaul relief programme was to fall apart due to industrial unrest – B&I crews demanded the same conditions as their *St Columba* colleagues for the period they were to operate from Dun Laoghaire. Strike action followed; B&I's *Leinster* was prevented from crossing Dublin Bay to Dun Laoghaire and sailings were suspended for three days while the *St Columba* underwent a 24-hour dry-docking in Govan to renew her passenger certificates.

Having returned to service after her Govan visit, the *St Columba* was finally able to stand down for her £80,000 major refurbishment early in April 1986. In her place came the *St David* once again. Her move to Dover had not been welcomed by British Ferries' Belgian partners RMT, particularly after James Sherwood made it known that he expected his ship to take up 50 per cent of the total traffic into Ostend. By the end of 1985, Sealink was prohibited from using Ostend and the *St David* had been switched back to Irish waters taking up a permanent slot on the Stranraer to Larne service in January 1986.

Retiring from the *St Columba* in September 1986 was Captain Len Evans after over forty-eight years at sea, twenty-five of which were in command – making him the most senior master in the Sealink fleet. A young Len Evans began his seagoing career in 1938 as a midshipman with Blue Funnel Line. On 10 October 1942, whilst on a voyage from Karachi to England, his ship, the *Agapenor*, picked up survivors from the torpedoed Glasgow ship *Glendene*. However, the following day the *Agapenor* was herself torpedoed by U-87 some 200 miles south-west of Freetown, Sierra Leone. Apart from seven crew members who perished, the ship's company were all picked up by the Royal Navy flower-class corvette *Petunia* – over 100 survivors, less than three days after the little corvette had rescued 250 survivors from the Blue Star ship *Andulacia Star*. During a voyage from Trincomalee to Calcutta, Len Evans was again sunk when the Japanese submarine I-165 slammed four torpedoes into Blue Funnel's *Perseus* off Madras, India on 16 January 1944. Capt G. G. Rumble and his crew were all saved, being rescued by a Royal Indian Navy corvette. After the war and still with Blue Funnel, a company affectionately known as the Welsh Navy, the twenty-year-old obtained his Master's Ticket in February 1948, but not before escaping serious injury when the ship in which he was serving struck a mine off Singapore in 1947. Returning to Holyhead to join British Railways in 1948, his first command was on the *Slieve Bloom* and his first passenger command came in 1966 when he became Master of the *Hibernia*. Replacing Captain Evans as Senior Master on the *St Columba* was Captain William Carroll, who in turn was succeeded on his own retirement in 1988 by Captain John Bakewell.

The relationship between B&I Line and Sealink British Ferries was further strained in April 1987 when the latter introduced the freight ship *Stena Sailer* to supplement sailings of *St Columba*. B&I cried foul and by the end of the year the partnership was at an end. It was business as usual and competition returned to Holyhead.

The *St David* returned to Holyhead for the overhaul relief again in April 1988. Unfortunately, she suffered an engine room fire while loading alongside at Dun Laoghaire one Sunday morning. For a time the Chief Engineer was missing, until rescued by the local fire brigade. The fire was caused by a fractured fuel line and forced an early withdrawal from service for repairs before she returned to the Stranraer station. Sealink hurriedly arranged a replacement charter in the form of the Isle of Man Steam Packet Company's side-loading car ferry *Mona's Queen*, pending the return of the *St Columba* from her refit. The Steam Packet's ro-ro vessel *Peveril* was also briefly drafted in to assist in moving the backlog of freight, as was Sealink's *Earl William*, which was about to open a new Liverpool–Dun Laoghaire route on 25 April.

The year 1988 saw quite a number of visitors to the Holyhead service. The start of the year also saw the *Earl Harold* (ex-*Ailsa Princess*) operating in place of the *Stena Sailer* for a period. Having finished that task, she was then placed on the Dun Laoghaire passenger service for three days from 11 February 1988 while the *St Columba* underwent an engine repair. Then came the *Vortigern* right at the very end of her Sealink career. Having been laid up at Chatham in Kent pending disposal, she was reactivated by Captain Trevor Shaw and his crew for operation on the Dun Laoghaire freight service on 7 March following an engine failure in the *Stena Sailer*. Arriving at Holyhead two days later, the ship made her first crossing to Dun Laoghaire on 10 March. The *Vortigern* was deprived of the opportunity to operate on the passenger service, and after the 0215 sailing to Dun Laoghaire on 31 March, she returned to

Holyhead in ballast under the command of Captain Tudor Jones. There she was handed over to her new Greek owners, Lindos Line, and renamed *Milos Express*.

An unusual development at Holyhead for a few weeks during the summer of 1988 was a Manx government service to and from the Isle of Man. Fred Olsen Lines' *Bolette* was taken on charter by the government, who were fearful of losing Isle of Man Steam Packet Company sailings during the busy TT Races period due to a seafarers strike. In the event, the strike ended, but not before it was too late to cancel the charter. The ship sailed from the Admiralty Pier between 26 May and 12 June providing Holyhead with its first scheduled Isle of Man car ferry route!

In a move to further develop the Holyhead ro-ro service, Sealink replaced the *Stena Sailer* with the significantly larger *Seafreight Highway* for the 1988 summer season, the smaller ship moving south to Fishguard to serve the Rosslare run. The 'Highway' was not a huge success on the route, primarily due to the fact that she really was a deep-sea ship and therefore fast turnarounds were difficult. It came as no surprise when the *Stena Sailer* returned to her Holyhead slot at the end of summer and before year end she had been purchased and renamed *St Cybi*. In January 1989 B&I brought in the chartered Sally Line ferry *The Viking* to provide overhaul relief on the Dublin–Holyhead service. Sealink's *Saint Eloi* was another visitor to Holyhead, taking up service on 4 April 1989, allowing the *St Columba* off for overhaul. The French-flagged ship was, to put it mildly, a mess, forcing the cancellation of her first round trip to Dun Laoghaire. Having been cleaned up, complaints about her dull and spartan appearance began flooding in and on one passage sixteen protesting passengers staged a 'sit-in' in the Master's cabin. When the *St Columba* returned on 27 April there was a collective sigh of relief. The *Saint Eloi* was dispatched to dry dock at Falmouth for a much-needed refit, from which she emerged renamed *Channel Entente*.

The steady growth in ro-ro traffic on the Irish Sea influenced container volumes and by the early 1980s the Belfast route was being particularly affected. The end finally came in 1989 when the *Rhodri Mawr* made the last Sealink Holyhead–Dublin–Belfast container sailings on 21 December. Some 1,250,000 containers had been carried since the service began in 1971 and between them the *Rhodri Mawr* and the *Brian Boroime* had made over 18,000 crossings of the Irish Sea. A replacement container service to Dublin, with the Freightliner contract, was opened by Maritime Transport Services with a container ship named *Rita*. This service however was later switched to the Mersey and Holyhead's container terminal became redundant. This was a bitter blow to the town as it followed the closure of the port's dry dock and marine workshops in 1986. Here had been a huge source of technical expertise and resources and during the twentieth century it had been the biggest employer of men in the town. The main workshops were located alongside the Refit Berth and a wide range of ship repairs, modifications and survey requirements were handled with ease over the years. However, a hallmark of the 1970s and 1980s was a lack of investment in the port's infrastructure, and with increasing ship sizes, the days of the dry dock were numbered.

On 31 January 1990, with 199 passengers on board, the *St Columba* was twelve miles west of the South Stack and inbound to Holyhead when an engine room fire occurred just after 11.30 a.m. Within seconds of the fire alarm warning, the senior engine room watchkeeper, 3rd Engineer Keith Jones, shut off the fuel supply and switched off the engines. His prompt reaction averted what could have become a much more serious situation. Senior Master Captain John Bakewell issued a 'Mayday' and passengers were mustered at boat stations in lifejackets. Holyhead lifeboat was launched and helicopters from 22 Squadron, RAF Valley, were alerted for a possible evacuation. B&I Line's *Leinster*, under the command of Captain Peter Pope, stood by all day to assist if required. Wearing breathing apparatus, the *St Columba*'s Working Party Red fire team of eighteen engine room and deck personnel tackled the blaze through dense smoke in the area of the port engine room turbo blower – and a minor fire in the funnel casing. The blaze was under control inside twenty minutes and extinguished by the crew within thirty minutes. The fourteen Gwynedd firemen airlifted to the ship by 22 Squadron then assisted in mopping-up operations. Although she was drifting without power, evacuation of the *St Columba* was not necessary, as south-west winds gradually took her further offshore. Captain Bakewell recalled the incident:

I wouldn't describe the Force 11 conditions as comfortable for our passengers in those circumstances, but there was absolutely no drama and everyone reacted extremely well.

Unfortunately with so much oil around it was deemed to be unsafe to attempt to restart the port engine. A tug from Holyhead was sent for, also firemen from Holyhead.

When the tug was made fast in appalling weather we began the tow towards Holyhead. We were only making one knot for the first few hours but eventually arrived off the breakwater. A very real danger was getting caught in the ebb tide when off South Stack. So course and speed (what there was of it) had to be adjusted so that we would get the benefit of the flood tide off the Stacks.

Norman Williams, our Purser, did a fine job looking after our passengers. We had very little smoke getting into the accommodation because fans had been turned off and fire shutters in position.

It was a great relief to berth at Salt Island around midnight. I berthed her bow in where it was still possible to discharge cars. Fortunately the bow thrust was working OK!

The cause was really a design fault. Our 3rd Engineer did really well in shutting down the oil flow immediately and all my crew did a great job. The only injury was to a fireman who broke his arm and the others were seasick!

The whole incident was marked by the absence of panic on board, and a situation, which was potentially extremely negative, in fact drew nothing but commendations for the manner in which it was handled, the matter receiving mention in Parliament:

1st February 1990
Mr. Ieuan Wyn Jones (Ynys Mon): I am sure that the Leader of the House and the House will be aware that the Sealink ship, the *St. Columba*, was badly damaged by fire in the Irish sea yesterday. The emergency services undertook excellent work; of the

294 people on board, only one received minor injuries. Will he and the House join me in thanking the emergency services which included the coastguards, the fire service, the RAF at Valley, the social services department, the Women's Royal Voluntary Service, trauma counsellors, the Samaritans, police and all the others who worked so hard to minimise the injuries? He will also be aware that Sealink is conducting its own inquiry to discover the cause of the fire. Will he assure us that, if necessary, the Department of Transport will also undertake an inquiry to find out whether regulations need to be tightened to prevent such incidents? Will he pass on that message, and the congratulations of the House on the work done by the emergency services, to the appropriate Secretary of State?

Sir Geoffrey Howe: I am sure that the whole House would wish me to join the hon. Gentleman in expressing our appreciation of the work carried out by the emergency services which he identified so comprehensively. I shall bring the other matter that he raised to the attention of my right hon. Friend the Secretary of State for Transport. There are virtually routine arrangements to ensure that such matters are considered as a matter of course.

A statement was also made in the House of Lords:

> Lord Cledwyn of Penrhos: My Lords, may I take this opportunity to pay a warm tribute to Captain Bakewell and the crew of the *St Columba* in Holyhead for the prompt and skilful way in which they dealt with the unfortunate accident? Their actions ensured that the passengers were not placed at risk.

A temporary replacement for the *St Columba* arrived in the form of Stranraer's *Darnia*, however she proved to be totally unsuitable and having completed just two round trips over a five-day period due to gales she was quickly returned to Scotland. In her place came the chartered Isle of Man Steam Packet side-loader *Lady of Mann*, which did sterling working maintaining the link through appalling weather conditions. She in turn was replaced in March by the *Horsa*, from Folkestone, newly allocated as a second seasonal passenger ship on the route following the closure of the short-lived Liverpool–Dun Laoghaire crossing.

Previously, a delegation from Holyhead travelled to Folkestone on 26 February to see the *Horsa*. It was the day of the floods along the North Wales coast and at Towyn in particular. Spray was being blown over the train as the track passed close to the sea and quips were made amongst the Sealink officers about lifejackets. The severity of the situation was not realised until an announcement at Chester that there would be no further trains into North Wales that day. The train carrying the delegation was the only train into London Euston because the diesel engine was kept on and not exchanged for an electric engine at Crewe as was the norm. The following day saw the *Horsa* stormbound in Calais but she eventually arrived in Folkestone and the Holyhead Officers were able to inspect the ship that evening and make a round trip to Boulogne in her the day after. After her initial relief work at Holyhead, the *Horsa* officially took up service in her new role on 23 May, reintroducing a seasonal two-ship passenger service to Dun Laoghaire. She was a popular and happy addition to the service and to give her an Irish Sea 'feel' many of her lounges were named after Welsh and Irish towns and regions.

Swedish Takeover

Following Sealink's acquisition by Stena Line on 31 May 1990 a massive fleet-wide investment programme was announced. This provided for significant extra capacity on the Irish Sea routes and included the return of the *Horsa* to Folkestone in October and the introduction in 1991 of a second year-round, multi-purpose ferry on the Holyhead run – the *Stena Cambria*, formerly the Dover flagship *St Anselm*.

Captain John Bakewell retired as the *St Columba*'s Senior Master in 1991. John left the Thames Nautical College HMS *Worcester* at the end of 1947 obtaining First Class Extra Certificates in school work and seamanship. On 16 January 1948, he joined Shaw Savill's *Coptic* as one of three cadets. At the end of three years apprenticeship, he took his 2nd Mate's Certificate and stayed on with Shaw Savill's to join the *Dominion Monarch* as Junior 4th Officer. Having stayed with Shaw Savill for nearly ten years he left them as 2nd Officer with a Master's certificate. John then joined HMS *Worcester* as 3rd Officer, staying there for six months before joining British Railway's ships in Holyhead in 1958, his first ship being the *Slieve Bloom*. His first command was the *Slieve Donard*.

As part of the investment programme, the *St Columba* sailed to Germany, under the command of new Senior Master Captain Trevor Salmon, for an £8 million refit, designed to transform her into a floating leisure centre in line with Stena's 'Travel Service Concept', which held that given top class ships, a wide range of facilities, quality entertainment and good value prices, then people would be encouraged to travel all year round, simply for the fun of the on-board experience. The *St Columba* was the first ship in the fleet to be so treated and returned to service with a new name and a very new look. As the *Stena Hibernia*, she provided a huge range of facilities including an à la carte restaurant and self service restaurant, a Pizza Factory, a Show Bar with resident band and visiting cabaret, an Irish Bar with traditional Irish music, Business Club and Conference Centre, Casino, Children's Play Area and, of course, well-stocked duty free and gift shops.

While the adoption of the name 'Hibernia' evoked a venerable past on the Holyhead route, the refit did not always meet with total approval from the travelling public. The renaming was an attempt to honour a long tradition going back almost a century and a half when the first *Hibernia* arrived at Holyhead. The *Stena Cambria*'s first task was to relieve the *St Columba* for her rebuild, but she had not been in service long when she had to be withdrawn for attention. In her place on 12 February 1991 came the renamed *Stena Horsa*, on passage back to Folkestone from overhaul at Birkenhead. The ship made two round trips before leaving Holyhead for the last time. At the very end of her career the *Cambridge Ferry* once again found herself in service to Dun Laoghaire. Next came the sale-listed *Earl William*. The old girl was in a sorry state following the closure of her Liverpool route one year previously, her rust-streaked hull devoid of any company markings and handling affected due to a faulty bow thrust unit. When the *Stena Cambria* returned to service on 19 February, the 'William' and the 'Cambridge' stood down. Under the command of Captain Ray Veno, the veteran train ferry sailed direct from Dun Laoghaire to Stranraer where upon arrival she commenced her final spell of Sealink service. One month later, the twenty-eight-year-old ship was laid up at Milford Haven pending sale to Italian owners.

The *Earl William* returned to her hibernation; however, she was reactivated again a few months later for the height of Holyhead's summer season when the *Stena Cambria* was delayed from relief duties at Dover. The ship was given a much-needed facelift prior to taking up service between Holyhead and Dun Laoghaire on 29 June 1991. On 8 July, the *Stena Cambria* finally arrived at her new home port releasing the *Earl William* for lay-up pending sale. Nine months later, she was sold for further trade.

The arrival of the *Stena Cambria* brought the inevitable end of the *St Cybi*, which was sold, although she was kept on for the 1991 season. However, her presence was missed in 1992 and to fill the gap for one month as freight traffic grew came the time-chartered German ro-ro *Auersberg*. Previously, the *Stena Hengist*, at the end of an illustrious Dover Strait career, appeared during January, coverning freight sailings with one daily round trip during the overhauls of the *Stena Hibernia* and the *Stena Cambria*. The year also saw the *Stena Galloway* from Stranraer in service at Holyhead when the *Stena Cambria* went off with gearbox trouble. And before year end another French ship – the *Chartres*, in lieu of the *Stena Cambria* during November.

From time to time, ships on the Dun Laoghaire service have had to delay sailings due to weather conditions. The days of sailing 'whatever the weather' with passengers spending a miserable night at sea did nothing to win custom for the operator. At Holyhead, it was often the case that sailings were delayed not due to the weather outside, but for the safety of the large ship leaving the confines of the Victorian port. The *Stena Hibernia*'s stern-first departure from the Station Berth in a southerly gale could be quite hairy, and there was a grudging admiration for the slightly shorter B&I ships, which used to do a free swing in the harbour.

Swinging stern on the quay was of course commonplace with the old cargo ships which would berth bow in at the Import Berth and which would then breast over with ropes to the Export Berth. They would then swing bow out, usually stern on the quay, but bow on in northerly winds. It was also common practice to swing the *Stena Hibernia*, when she was the *St Columba,* on the quay at the Refit Berth when the needs of the refit required, but it was not done in a southerly gale!

With the arrival of the *Stena Cambria*, the difference in available power in such conditions was noticeable. It became apparent to the *Stena Hibernia*'s Captain Richard 'Bwana' Jones that if they failed to sail then the 'Cambria' might well have to wait outside the port until the weather moderated. This prompted Captain Jones to look for a solution, as he explains:

After studying the charts for many a long hour and visiting the Container Terminal I realised that by landing the stern of the ship and pinning it on one set of piles on the container berth there was just sufficient space to swing the ship there, allowing us to proceed out of the harbour bow first.

At the time I was sailing as Night Master with Captain Ian Farrell as the Day Master. I think I had been talking to him for some time about the possibility of this manoeuvre when one day it was blowing a strong gale from the south. The Refit Berth was occupied, the *Stena Cambria* was outside the port with nowhere to go and I was in bed while Ian was preparing for the afternoon sailing. The next thing I was put on the shake as I was wanted on the bridge where I was told, 'This is your bloody idea, so we'll do it together.'

After a bit of a conflab we put the idea into practice and lo and behold the birth of the 'Bwana Swing'.

Over time this method was much improved upon, but it could only be performed if tidal conditions were absolutely right and as the piles on the container berth were somewhat small, landing and keeping the stern on them was quite tricky. Although the container service had finished the cranes were still in position, which on a few occasions nearly caused the old adrenalin to flow!! I am not sure how many Masters used this manoeuvre – Captain Ian Farrell and I did it regularly and Captain Hugh Farrell did it at least a couple of times.

And the name 'Bwana'? Before joining the Holyhead ships I was working as a surveyor in West Africa, so I was named 'Dick Bwana' by some wag on the *Slieve Donard*. Actually, the title 'Bwana' is from East Africa, but what the hell – Holyhead folk have never allowed a few thousand miles of geographical error to stand in the way of a good nickname!!

The *Stena Hibernia*'s Senior Master Captain Trevor Salmon retired in 1993 after thirty-two years of service at Holyhead. Over the years, Trevor had many experiences including the inaugural sailing of the *Holyhead Ferry I* and taking the *Seafreight Highway* on sea trials off the coast of Greece. Another was, for three years running, bringing the dredger *Landguard* to Holyhead from Harwich. However, the ship closest to Trevor's heart was his last. And rightly so, for as the *St Columba* he was on her delivery trip from Aalborg in 1977 and later oversaw the Stena Line conversion of the ship in Bremerhaven.

Also 'retiring' in 1993 was the *Stena Cambria*'s Senior Master, Captain Tudor Jones. Tudor comes from a family with port connections dating back to 1853. Growing up watching all the ships working from Holyhead in the 1950s at very close quarters as they berthed and dry-docked a mere ship's length or two from the family home, a career at sea was an obvious choice and, in 1956, he went to sea as a midshipman with Blue Funnel after passing out of HMS *Conway*. Returning to Holyhead, he joined British Rail continuing the family tradition – his father Gwilym Jones (who had supervised the building of the *Slieve Donard* and the *Holyhead Ferry 1*) was at the time Chief Engineer, while his uncle, Captain Ivor Griffiths, was Master on the *Hibernia* and the *Cambria*. Despite 'retiring', Captain Jones is still very much involved with the Holyhead scene, serving as Pilot and also sitting on the local pilotage committee.

An aerial view of the *St David*, June 1985. (Justin Merrigan Collection)

Holyhead No. 7 berth and station platforms. (Justin Merrigan Collection)

The dry dock at Holyhead. (Justin Merrigan Collection)

The *St Columba* passes the *Vortigern* in dry dock at Holyhead in February 1985. (Justin Merrigan Collection)

The *Saint Eloi* at Admiralty Pier on 25 April 1989. (Captain Ray Veno)

The *Brian Boroime* sails from Holyhead with a full load of containers. (W. Owen Williams)

The container vessel *Rhodri Mawr* sails from Holyhead. (W. Owen Williams)

Presentation to Captain Len Evans, retiring Senior Master of the *St Columba*, September 1986.

The *Bolette* leaves Holyhead for Douglas, Isle of Man, on 12 June 1988. (Captain Ray Veno)

The Isle of Man Steam Packet vessel *Peveril* helping out at Dun Laoghaire, April 1988. (Justin Merrigan)

The Isle of Man Steam Packet car ferry *Mona's Queen* at Dun Laoghaire.

The *Stena Sailer* at the Carlisle Pier in 1987. (Justin Merrigan)

B&I Line's *Leinster* at Holyhead in September 1988. (Judi and Lee Brown)

The *Stena Horsa*. (Nigel Thornton Collection)

Sally Line's *The Viking,* on charter to B&I Line, February 1989. (Captain Ray Veno)

The *Earl Harold* at Holyhead on 4 April 1988. (Captain Ray Veno)

The *St Cybi* arrives at Dun Laoghaire. (Justin Merrigan)

A stormy crossing to Belfast for the *Rhodri Mawr*. (W. Owen Williams)

The *Vortigern* lays over at Dun Laoghaire's St Michael's Pier days before withdrawal from service. (Justin Merrigan)

A stern view of the *Horsa*, alongside the station at Holyhead. (Judi and Lee Brown)

Her Sealink career nearly over, the *St Cybi* rests at Holyhead, seen from the *Stena Cambria*. (Justin Merrigan)

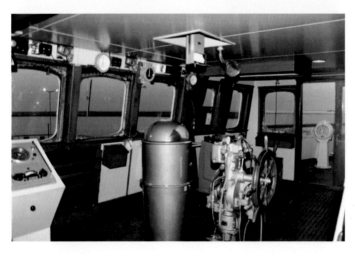

The bridge on the *Cambridge Ferry*. (Justin Merrigan)

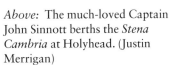

Above: The much-loved Captain John Sinnott berths the *Stena Cambria* at Holyhead. (Justin Merrigan)

Top right: The *Seafreight Highway* berths at the Admiralty Pier at Holyhead. (Justin Merrigan)

Middle right: The *Stena Cambria* in 1991. (Justin Merrrigan)

Bottom right: The *Earl William* at Dun Laoghaire in June 1991. (Justin Merrigan)

The *St Columba* passes
fishing boats as she sails
from Holyhead. (Ian
Collard)

The *Stena Galloway* at
Dun Laoghaire in August
1992. (Justin Merrigan)

The *Stena Cambria*
arrives at Holyhead. (Ian
Collard)

The *Stena Cambria* passes a small naval vessel as she arrives at Holyhead. (Ian Collard)

The *Stena Hibernia* moves astern out of Holyhead on her departure to Dun Laoghaire. (Ian Collard)

The chartered *Isle of Innisfree* berthed at Holyhead. (Dick Richards)

B&I Line's Rosslare vessel
the *Munster* appeared at
Holyhead on overhaul
relief. (Gordon Hislip)

B&I Line's *Leinster* mid-
passage to Holyhead.
(Justin Merrigan)

The *Norröna* in service at
Dun Laoghaire in February
1994. (Justin Merrigan)

9

Embracing the Future

Just seven weeks before a scheduled inauguration, Stena Sealink Line announced their entry into the fledgling high-speed car ferry sector. Cutting the crossing time between Holyhead and Dun Laoghaire from 3 hours 30 minutes to 110 minutes, the Tasmanian-built Incat 74-metre Wave Piercing Catamaran *Stena Sea Lynx* entered service on 16 July 1993. The craft had left Hobart on 9 June, calling en route at Cairns, Darwin, Singapore, Colombo, Djibouti and then up the Red Sea to the Suez Canal. Joining her in Malta for the homeward leg to the Irish Sea was Captain Hugh Farrell, who would become her Senior Master. With a dedicated crew, Captain Farrell considered the 'Lynx' to be the highlight of his career. Being at the forefront of technology the craft introduced a whole new way of doing business. Many of the traditional ship-handling skills had to be put aside as waterjets and steering buckets replaced propellers and rudders. And being so light, when compared with a conventional ferry, had a significant effect on berthing. The ship management structure comprised a Master, Chief Engineer, Navigator – all based on the craft's bridge. An Assistant Engineer remained in the engine room and four deck crew tied up the craft and loaded the car deck.

In the passenger 'cabin' a totally different image was created for passengers. Crew training was brought in using people experienced in the airline industry and this was then continued through company trainers. Little surprise then that the passenger services structure was more comparable to an airline than a ferry, with a cabin manager in overall charge of an assistant manager and 10/12 cabin assistants. The assistants could be assigned to any area including the shop, bar or café and their duties also included cleaning the craft on turnaround and demonstrating safety procedures before departure.

For passenger comfort Stena Sealink did not operate the 'Lynx' in waves above 3.5 metres significant height and a wind speed of Force 7. In such cases, passengers were contacted and diverted to the *Stena Hibernia* and *Stena Cambria*. They were also issued with information packs, a meal voucher and a phone card. Indeed, all connected with the service went through a very fast learning curve. That the ports were prepared and the service was up and running in just seven weeks was a tremendous effort, a combination of hard work and team work under then Shipping and Port Manager Colin Hetherington.

No sooner had the *Stena Sea Lynx* arrived in Holyhead from Hobart than Stena Sealink Line announced even greater things to come; the High-speed Sea Service, or HSS. That the £65 million order for the first of a series of these giant catamarans was placed for the Holyhead service was a huge show of Stena's confidence in the Irish Sea route. The gas turbine vessel, travelling at twice the speed of conventional ferries, delivered a revolution, according to Stena Line Board Chairman Dan Sten Olsson, not seen since air travel moved from the propeller to the jet age. To accommodate the HSS, major civil engineering works were undertaken on both sides of the Irish Sea; at Holyhead, the new facility was located on the site of the former container terminal, while, at Dun Laoghaire, the car ferry terminal at St Michael's Wharf was completely redeveloped.

Meanwhile, during the *Stena Sea Lynx*'s first six months in service, the total market on the route grew by over 200,000 passengers and 40,000 cars. With capacity for 425 passengers and eighty cars, the immediate success of *Stena Sea Lynx* led Stena Sealink Line to acquire the larger 78-metre vessel *Stena Sea Lynx II* in 1994, the smaller craft moving south to Fishguard to launch a high-speed operation there.

The *Stena Hibernia*'s new Senior Master, Captain John Garner, was seconded to the Stena HSS project team responsible for the design, construction and build of the new craft in Finnyards. Taking over as Acting Senior Master was Captain Richard Jones, who, as it turned out, would be the ship's final local Senior Master. Richard joined British Rail at Holyhead in 1972, his first ship being the *Slieve Donard*. Over the years he sailed on most ships that served on the Holyhead route to Ireland, gaining his first command on the container ship *Brian Boroime* in 1989. Two years later, his first passenger command came in the form of the *Earl William*.

An interesting visitor in 1994 was the Faroese-flag *Norröna* on a three-month charter to Stena Sealink Line to cover overhaul periods on both the Fishguard and Holyhead routes. Her time at Holyhead was primarily in a freight role sailing on the *Stena Cambria*'s schedules.

While all of this was going on B&I Line was also going through radical change. The company was sold by the Irish government to Irish Continental Group (ICG) on 1 January 1992, bringing much needed investment in tonnage to their Irish Sea routes. One of their first acts was to transfer their chartered *Isle of Innisfree* from Rosslare to Dublin for the Holyhead service in 1993. However, the move was unsuccessful in that she was a touch too slow for the run and also experienced difficulties when berthing in adverse weather. The ship was returned to Rosslare to complete her charter. In readiness for the May 1995 arrival of the first newbuild for the Irish since the *Leinster* of 1981, ICG's Irish Ferries brand was extended to the former B&I routes and for the first time the Irish service was now able to compete with the Stena Sealink operation on a level playing field. The move saw the *Leinster* take a new name: *Isle of Inishmore*.

January 1995 brought Stranraer's *Stena Antrim* into service at Holyhead, covering for the overhaul periods of the *Stena Cambria* and the *Stena Hibernia* fourteen years after she unexpectedly had her maiden voyage on the service as the *St Christopher*. Following Irish Ferries' transfer of the *Isle of Inishmore* to Rosslare, the company's *Saint Patrick II* was allocated to the Dublin–Holyhead service from 8 March pending the arrival of the new *Isle of Innisfree*. Unfortunately, a small fire broke out in the

'Paddy' ten days later, forcing her withdrawal to Birkenhead for repairs. Sailings were cancelled for four days until the *Isle of Inishmore* could be brought back to Dublin where she remained until the new ship arrived. This had been the *Saint Patrick II*'s second stint at Holyhead, the first being in 1984 on charter to B&I Line for overhaul relief.

Probably one of the most eagerly awaited events in Irish maritime history took place on 23 May 1995 when the *Isle of Innisfree* (II) entered service to Holyhead. At 181 metres long the ship was impressive. Her speed at 21.5 knots was almost 20 per cent faster than the chartered ship of the same name. Another historic moment was the closure of the station berth on 2 June. The *Stena Hibernia* started operating from Holyhead's original car ferry berth at Salt Island and, after she sailed for Dun Laoghaire at 2.15 p.m., she was followed in by the *Stena Cambria*.

While the spotlight was trained on preparations for the coming HSS service, another newcomer started working, out of the limelight, early in November 1995. The *Stena Traveller*, under Senior Master Captain David Farrell, was also a key element in the company's quest to revamp travel on the Holyhead routes. With capacity in excess of 100 articulated trucks the *Stena Traveller* replaced the *Stena Cambria* but running to Dublin Port instead of Dun Laoghaire. This gave hauliers their own dedicated freight ship, a move welcomed by some Dun Laoghaire residents who were concerned about the increase in ro-ro traffic through their town.

The replacement of the *Stena Cambria* by the new ship didn't go as smoothly as Stena Sealink Line would have liked. During her evening sailing to Dun Laoghaire on 5 October, the *Stena Cambria*'s port engine was found to be running hot due to a loss of lube oil. With gale conditions prevailing, the engine was shut down and berthing at the Irish port was aided by a tug. An inspection by divers revealed a wire wrapped around her port shaft causing seal damage. With winds gusting to Force 10, the *Stena Cambria* limped from Dun Laoghaire bound for dry dock in Birkenhead. In her place on the Dun Laoghaire run five days later came the chartered *Marine Evangeline*, maintaining freight sailings until the opening of the Dublin service.

At the end of the year, the much-respected Sealink brand was dropped – the company now trading under the name of its Swedish parent, Stena Line. The *Stena Hibernia* returned to Holyhead from overhaul at Swansea not only wearing the new Stena Line livery, but also carrying a new name: *Stena Adventurer*.

Delays during the construction of the HSS meant inauguration of the new service in time for the 1995 summer season failed to materialise and the launch was put back to 1996. However, the biggest redevelopment of the port since Telford and Rennie transformed it in the nineteenth century was completed in January 1996. The new £5 million link bridge, which closed off the station berth, connecting the east and west sides of the Inner Harbour, was opened two months previously. The bridge was seen as an essential link in the free movement of traffic in the port, which now had all vehicle check-in facilities located together at the entrance to what had been the container terminal. Dun Laoghaire too underwent significant change in readiness for the arrival of the HSS. Designed along airport lines to process passengers quickly and effortlessly, the new terminal at St Michael's Pier was surrounded by a large landscaped plaza with seating, palm trees and a fountain. Vertical emphasis was by way of a glazed circular tower rising from the centre of the building and a projecting stone wall positioned to create a dialogue with both the old Town Hall and the railway station buildings – helping to enclose the plaza. The building continues to use a nautical theme throughout – porthole windows and decking feature, as do large areas of glazing, brise-soleils, and metal panelling. The ticket booths for vehicular access were given weather protection by large membrane structures designed to remind of the heyday of sail and Dun Laoghaire's great maritime heritage.

A further last-minute delay with the HSS brought another brief visitor to the service over Easter 1996 in the form of the chartered Newhaven–Dieppe ferry *Stena Londoner*. She was pressed into service at the eleventh hour, working with the *Stena Adventurer* and the *Stena Lynx*, and, in so doing, became the last ship to carry the Sealink brand on the Irish Sea.

For the *Stena Explorer*'s delivery voyage from Finland to the UK, under the command of Senior Master Captain Andy Humphreys, Stena Line could not have wished for better weather conditions – NE Force 9-10 winds in the North Sea. She performed magnificently. Indeed, on arrival at Holyhead on 21 February, a piece of unsecured timber, which had been used as a fender, was still in place resting on her transom! In service, her Maritime & Coastguard Agency Permit to Operate restricted her operation to waves of up to four metres significant height.

The General Electric-manufactured gas turbines on the *Stena Explo*rer were rebuilt for maritime use, with each of the two hulls containing two types, one large and one small. The larger develops approximately 30,000 horsepower at 3,600 rpm, while the smaller develops approximately 20,000 horsepower at 6,500 rpm. The maritime versions of the gas turbines are powered by a light diesel oil with a very low sulphur content. The gas turbines, including the power turbines, are completely encased in fire and soundproof containers, known as turbine modules. The HSS takes much of its technology from the world of aviation. The smaller of the two types of gas turbines are used in the Swedish Air Force's fighter, attack and reconnaissance aircraft, the Saab Gripen, while the larger of the two types is used in the long-haul Boeing 747 aircraft. There are several reasons why Stena's designers elected to use aircraft-engine-type gas turbines as the power source. They produce cleaner exhaust fumes than conventional diesel engines, require less space, weigh less, have a high level of operational reliability and are virtually vibration-free. However, they are also incredibly thirsty engines, something that troubled the craft ten years later.

In narrow waters, the HSS 1500 can be powered by the two smaller engine packages, giving a maximum speed of 25 knots. When the larger modules are in operation, the vessel has an approximate top speed of 32 knots, and when all four modules are operating at full power, the ferry's speed can exceed 40 knots.

A new docking technique to speed loading and unloading, as well as a system for storing supplies, were among the unique features of the *Stena Explorer*, enabling her to be turned around, re-stored and refuelled in just thirty minutes, if required. The linkspan for the HSS was a completely new design, which also includes a quick coupling with fuel, fresh water and waste water pipes. When the HSS docks, she reverses in towards the linkspan. The reversing manoeuvre is made easier by the craft being fitted with differential GPS (which can determine her position to within one metre), four TV cameras, and a bow thruster in each hull. Once the HSS has made contact with the linkspan's fenders, the quick couplings are connected on either side of the ferry's stern, pulling it automatically into the correct position so that gangways and drive-on ramps fit. The ferry's massive beam and a specially constructed aft fender, which prevents the ship from moving sideways, mean no additional moorings, such as ropes, are required. Once berthed, rapid loading and unloading is achieved by using the ferry's four stern doors. Thanks to the beam, cars, coaches and trucks turn around on board in a wide U-turn. Three of the doors are used simultaneously during loading. Two of them lead into the ferry's main loading deck, while the third leads cars up to an extra pontoon deck situated above the main deck, via a ramp. Three doors are also used during unloading as vehicles drive through the 180-degree curve on board. Foot passengers go on board and ashore along two parallel passenger gangways, located on either side of the linkspan, so avoiding stairs and other barriers.

The *Stena Explorer* finally entered service on 10 April 1996 when she sailed from the Irish port at 6.53 a.m. under the command of Captain John Roberts. Her first day in service was greeted by perfect weather and some very busy crossings. Her second sailing from Dun Laoghaire saw 1,109 passengers and 223 cars loaded in little over ten minutes.

The arrival of the HSS concept on the Holyhead–Dun Laoghaire service numbered the former *St Columba*'s remaining days on the Irish Sea. In January 1996, the ship was earmarked for a transfer to Dover, where her high passenger capacity would have been welcomed. In the event, the *Stena Adventurer* remained at Holyhead beyond the entry into service of the *Stena Explorer*.

Boosting its position at Holyhead in face of Stena's expansion, Irish Ferries chartered in the ro-ro vessel *Purbeck* from Sally Line. Entering service in May, the ship provided an extra daily round trip between May and October, operating in support of the *Isle of Innisfree*. Having played support to the *Stena Explorer* during the summer season, the end for the conventional ferry service to Dun Laoghaire finally came on 30 September 1996. Having completed her final sailing, the *Stena Adventurer* was laid up at the Carlisle Pier and, for one month, the former flagship of the Sealink fleet remained on standby in the event of mechanical problems on the HSS. After this period of inactivity the ship was moved from Dun Laoghaire to Belfast for lay-up pending sale.

Before her move northwards, the former *St Columba* was permitted one final visit to her homeport, operating a round trip to clear a backlog of traffic on 29 October. The following evening, the *Stena Adventurer* slipped out of Dun Laoghaire under the command of Captain Jim Wilcox. As she left the harbour Stena Line's port vehicles lined the quay sounding their horns, a salute normally reserved for retiring masters. In response, the *Stena Adventurer*'s whistle echoed around Dun Laoghaire as she completed her final swing before heading into Dublin Bay. Eight hours later she arrived at Belfast, 'Finished with Engines' being rung off at 2.40 a.m. on 31 October.

On 5 April 1997, the twentieth anniversary of the *St Columba*'s departure from Aalborg on her delivery voyage to Holyhead, news broke of a possible sale to Agapitos

Express Ferries of Greece. On 9 May, renamed *Express Aphrodite*, the ship left Belfast and the Irish Sea for the last time. Meanwhile, the *Stena Cambria* was back at Holyhead providing overhaul relief for the HSS *Stena Explorer* and on 3 May she became the last conventional ferry to sail from Dun Laoghaire. The arrival of the *Stena Challenger* on the Dublin freight service in September 1996, replacing the *Stena Traveller*, opened the fledgling route to non-freight customers thanks to her ability to accommodate up to 500 passengers. This ability proved its worth during the winter months when adverse weather affected HSS sailings on the Dun Laoghaire run.

While all this was going on, the enormous success of Irish Ferries' Dutch-built *Isle of Innisfree* brought continued growth, to such an extent that an even larger ship was required. For this Irish Ferries turned to the Netherlands again and in 1997 the *Isle of Inishmore* entered service between Dublin and Holyhead, releasing the 'Innisfree' for service at Rosslare. Despite the ending of conventional services to Dun Laoghaire, the *Stena Cambria*'s association with Holyhead stretched out until March 1998. Devoid of Stena Line markings in readiness for a transfer to the newly created P&O Stena Line at Newhaven, the 'Cambria' found herself sailing to Dublin Port after the intended relief ship, *Stena Caledonia*, unexpectedly became unavailable. After service between Newhaven and Dieppe, the *Stena Cambria* was sold for service in Spanish waters in February 1999.

In 1999, Irish Ferries entered the fast craft arena with their Dublin Swift service and the catamaran *Jonathan Swift*. Built at a cost of IR£29 million, the *Jonathan Swift*'s speed of 39 knots reduced the crossing time from Dublin City to Holyhead to just 1 hour 49 minutes. The craft, which offers space for 800 passengers and 200 cars, arrived in Dublin after a twenty-three-day voyage from Western Australia on 5 May 1999. Under the command of Captains Tony Canavan, Steve Hutson and Paul Devaney, and with a complement of twenty crew, her route home was via the Indian Ocean, Suez Canal, Mediterranean and through the Bay of Biscay with stops along the way for refuelling. Boundaries were pushed even further in March 2001 as cut throat competition intensified. Taking up service for Irish Ferries was the giant *Ulysses*, all 50,938 gross tonnes of her, providing capacity for 1,875 passengers and a staggering 4,106 metres of vehicle space equivalent to 1,342 cars or 240 articulated lorries.

Providing overhaul relief for the *Stena Challenger* in December 1999 was the *Stena Invicta*, on charter from P&O Stena Line at Dover. The *Stena Challenger* remained at Holyhead until her sale to Canadian operators in April 2001 and in her place came the chartered Italian-flag *Stena Forwarder*. The ship was another boost for the service that started as a freight-only route. With accommodation for 1,000 passengers, 500 more than her predecessor, the *Stena Forwarder* also increased freight capacity by some 60 per cent. The 'Forwarder' was Stena's temporary answer to the *Ulysses* while new tonnage was being built in South Korea. Ordered at Hyundai Heavy Industries at a cost of £68 million, the new ship would increase passenger capacity on the Dublin Port route by 50 per cent and freight capacity by 70 per cent. The 211-metre vessel is three metres longer than the *Ulysses* and as such Stena Line made full use of the claim that she is the 'longest ferry ever to sail on the Irish Sea'. In fact, it was interesting to stand on board the *Stena Adventurer* and look down on the wheelhouse of the competitor. But while the *Stena Adventurer* may be longer and have a wheelhouse one deck higher, the *Ulysses* could still lay claim to being the largest car ferry, in terms of vehicle capacity, in the world.

With the arrival of the new *Stena Adventurer* in sight, the 'Forwarder' was sold by her Italian owners for service in Mexico. Her final sailing from Dublin was on 13 April 2003, by which time she had already been renamed *California Star*. Filling in, pending the delivery of the *Stena Adventurer*, was the *Stena Transporter* from Stena Line's North Sea services.

The arrival of the new ship into service on the Dublin crossing during July 2003 significantly improved Stena Line's position on the Irish Sea. Under the command of Captain Eric Davies, the ship had sailed from Korea on her delivery voyage, calling at Dublin for berthing trials before arriving in Holyhead for the first time on 16 June.

Driving on board the *Stena Adventurer* is quite an experience – her vehicle decks being best described as cavernous! The ship offers some 3,400 lane metres over decks 1, 3, 5 and 7. Access is through the bow and stern on two levels, decks 5 and 3, the latter having a 15-metre-long stern ramp and an 18-metre-long bow ramp. A tiltable ramp also connects deck 3 with deck 5 while a fixed ramp takes vehicles to deck 1, an area with 415 lane metres. As built, the ship accommodated 1,500 passengers on decks 7, 8 and 9, offering passengers first-class on-board facilities including cinema, casino, restaurants, lounges and children's play areas. A total of 364 passenger berths are also available in 148 luxury cabins. The ship's four MAN B&W diesel engines each provide 6,480 kW and provide a service speed of 22 knots. Twin KaMeWa bow thrusters are also fitted and this, together with her twin 65-degree-angle Becker rudders and twin controllable-pitch, high skew KaMeWa screws, make the *Stena Adventurer* a very manoeuvrable ship.

Under Stena Ports ownership Holyhead has seen a much-needed injection of capital. In 1993 the company embarked on heavy investment in associated facilities for the high-speed service being made over a three-year period. The introduction of the *Stena Adventurer* brought a second twin-tier berth to Holyhead at a cost of over £10 million.

For the tenth year of HSS operation Stena Line announced a revised timetable for the *Stena Explorer*. A decline in tourist volumes as a consequence of competition from low-cost airlines and other ferry operators and, more importantly, very high fuel costs, which had doubled in just 18 months, combined to force Stena Line to take action. The new order was for two HSS round trips a day, year round from 25 September 2006 with the flexibility to increase trips when needed. During the summer months a two-trip timetable operated on Monday–Thursday inclusive and a three-round-trip timetable on Friday, Saturday and Sunday.

During September 2006, Stena Line redeployed an existing ro-ro ferry from its North Sea fleet, the *Stena Seatrader*, to commence operations on the Dublin route. The new service completed one round trip per day, leaving Holyhead at 10.15 p.m. and Dublin at 3.15 p.m., increasing capacity on the corridor significantly. The additional ship came on the back of a successful year for Stena Line which saw total freight volumes grow by 8 per cent during 2005. The company's five Irish Sea routes were particularly successful enjoying growth of 16 per cent, with the biggest increase taking place on the Holyhead to Dublin Bay routes where the number of freight vehicles travelling on these routes jumped to 173,000 units.

Joining the Stena Line fleet at Holyhead in 2006 was the Damen Stan Tug *St David*; a happy choice of name, albeit a slightly smaller vessel than the last to honour the Welsh saint! Her main functions at the port centre on mooring, pushing and towing duties, but she has, from time to time, served as relief Pilot vessel. The *St David* has a length O.A. of 19.70 metres and a breadth O.A. of 6.38 metres. Draught (aft) is 2.65 metres and displacement is 138 tonnes. Owned by Stena Line Ports, she carries an MCA workboat code category 2, and is permitted to operate sixty miles from a safe haven. Speed is 11.7 knots and max bollard pull – full ahd – is 22.4 ton (m). Engines are 2 x Caterpillar 3412C TA/B while nozzles are 2 x 1,500-mm van de Giessen Optima.

As fuel costs soared to $147 for a barrel of crude, and the global economy went into freefall, a further reduction in the HSS service was announced in October 2008. With effect from 10 November, the ship's schedules fell to just one round trip per day, except for the Christmas and New Year holiday period when the vessel double tripped. In July 2008, Stena Line started accepting foot passengers on the Dublin service for the first time, news that coincided with a plan to slow down the *Stena Explorer* on the Dun Laoghaire crossing by sixteen minutes to save costs in the face of still-rising fuel prices. It should be remembered that when the *Stena Explorer* was designed, a barrel of crude cost in the region of $16. In October 2008, it was announced that the *Stena Nordica* would be transferred to the Irish Sea from her usual route between Sweden and Poland as a replacement for the *Stena Seatrader*. The ship commenced her new role on 12 November and, in March 2009, received a £2 millon refit and refurbishment to include new passenger lounges and bar, a new Stena Plus lounge, a Food City restaurant, a new freight drivers' area and refurbished seating and flooring.

The *Stena Adventurer* too received a £3.1 million refit in readiness for the 2009 season, including a complete revamp of deck 8 to include a new 202-seater Stena Plus lounge incorporating a family area with MSN stations and dedicated toilets, a new business area with WiFi, a Barista Coffee house, a new shop, a Teen Town branded area with MSN stations, a Met Bar & Grill, a Curious George Play Area and a quiet area/reading room.

Further economies were put in place for the 2010 HSS season. Replacing the *Stena Explorer* during the off-peak periods was the Incat 81-metre *Stena Lynx III*; the smaller craft allowing for a significantly more cost-effective operation and an opportunity to return the Dun Laoghaire route to profit. The *Stena Explorer* meanwhile was rostered to return for the peak summer season from 28 June to 5 September. During this period, the *Stena Lynx III* returned to Fishguard for her summer fast craft service to Rosslare. In the event, the *Stena Explorer* was pressed back into service earlier than planned following an increase in passenger traffic.

Before we close our work, we must mention the development of cruise ship traffic through the port of Holyhead. Cruise ships started calling at Holyhead on a more regular basis during the mid-1990s; however, the lack of dedicated berthing facilities for ships at the larger end of the scale saw the port lose out to Liverpool which had capitalised on its status of European Capital of Culture 2008 and the existence of significant European grant funds to build a brand-new cruise berth. Unwilling to accept this, the Welsh Assembly Government and Isle of Anglesey County Council combined with Stena Line Ports and Anglesey Aluminium (AAM) to work towards establishing Holyhead as the premier Welsh cruise liner destination. With this strong partnership securely in place work began on upgrading of the port's cruise offering. Captain Wyn Parry, head of port operations says,

> Holyhead has always been a popular cruise destination but in the last three or four years we have seen an increase in the number of ships that come here. We can deliver the plans and we are progressing down the route of developing a new dedicated deep water cruise berth capable of being easily accessed by the very largest modern day cruise ships.

In the meantime, with the co-operation of AAM, the existing jetty, which was operated until June 2009 to import dry bulk materials in the form of alumina and petroleum coke for their Penrhos Works in Holyhead, was modified to accommodate large cruise ships. On 7 August 2010, Holyhead welcomed the largest cruise ship ever to berth alongside at the port; the *Westerdam*. The ship made her approach to Holyhead at approximately 6.00 a.m., local Stena Pilots Captain Tudor Jones and Captain Tudor Roberts boarding the vessel some three miles out. As the *Westerdam* made her approach, the port's Pilot boat, the *St Cybi* and the port tug, the *St David*, stood off to watch her make her entrance. The *St David* then followed the *Westerdam* in as she made her final approach, to assist in berthing. It was a proud moment for all who have worked hard to establish Holyhead as a cruise destination. The 82,500-tonne *Westerdam*, a ten-deck ship, berthed alongside the new cruise terminal without so much as a bump. The berth had been refurbished for its new role and now offers a stage for performers, toilet facilities for coach drivers, information point – operated by volunteers from the local Maritime Museum – and a small internet suite for crew members to use. On board the *Westerdam* were a total of 1,968 passengers and 1,000 crew. They all received a colourful welcome from dancers and performers on the jetty, as well as an opportunity to enjoy a tour of Anglesey's many attractions.

Until 2010, larger vessels had to anchor outside the harbour and shuttle passengers ashore in tenders to the pontoons in the fish dock. The ship's visit marked a new milestone in the regeneration of Holyhead. And why not? Holyhead is ideally placed for the whole of the Irish Sea cruise market. The world-famous Snowdonia National Park is located only thirty miles away from the port. Caernarfon Castle is only forty minutes away by road!

The Port of Holyhead is a twenty-four-hours-a-day, deep-water port. With an alongside depth of 10.5 metres, large cruise ships are easily accommodated at the new Cruise Terminal. Couple this with the bustling ferry trade, numbering some sixty services per week, and one can see that Holyhead's future as the gateway to Ireland is secure.

PRINCIPAL FLEET LIST – vessels allocated to the Holyhead Station

Name	Holyhead service	Tonnage	Speed	Built
Scotia	1847-1861	479grt	14k	1847, Wigram & Co., London
Anglia	1847-1861	473grt	14k	1847, Ditchburn & Mare
Hibernia	1847-1878	573grt	14k	1847, Thomas Vernon & Sons, Liverpool
Cambria	1848-1884	590grt	14k	1848, Laird Brothers, Birkenhead
Ocean	1853-1862	507grt		1836, Mottishead & Hayes, Liverpool
Hercules	1853-1862	265grt		1838, Mottishead & Hayes, Liverpool
Queen	1853-1862			1838, Tod & MacGregor, Glasgow
Sea Nymph	1856-1878	685grt		1845, Caird & Company, Greenock
Telegraph	1856-1874	848grt	16k	1853, J. & G. Thomson, Govan
Admiral Moorsom	1860-1880	794grt	13k	1860, Randolph Elder & Company, Glasgow
Alexandra	1863-1889	703grt	13k	1863, Laird Brothers, Birkenhead
Stanley	1864-1888	782grt	13k	1864, Caird & Company, Greenock
Countess of Erne	1868-1873	825grt	13k	1868, Walpole, Webb & Company, Dublin
Duke of Sutherland	1868-1888	853grt	13k	1868, Andrew Leslie & Company, Hebburn
Duchess of Sutherland	1869-1888	893grt	13k	1869, Andrew Leslie & Company, Hebburn
Edith	1870-1892	758grt	13k	1870, Andrew Leslie & Company, Hebburn

Eleanor	1876-1892	917grt	13k	1873, Robert Stephenson & Company, Newcastle
Rose	1876-1894	1,177grt	20k	1876, Laird Brothers, Birkenhead
Shamrock	1875-1898	1,178grt	20k	1876, Laird Brothers, Birkenhead
Earl Spencer	1877-1896	855grt		1874, Laird Brothers, Birkenhead
Isabella	1877-1898	855grt		1877, Laird Bothers, Birkenhead
Lily	1880-1900	1,035grt	17 ½k	1880, Laird Brothers, Birkenhead
Violet	1880-1902	1,035grt	17 ½k	1880, Laird Brothers, Birkenhead
Banshee	1884-1906	1,035grt	17 ½k	1884, Laird Brothers, Birkenhead
Eleanor	1881-1902	854grt	17k	1881, Laird Brothers, Birkenhead
Holyhead	1883	931grt	15k	1883, Robert Duncan & Company, Port Glasgow
North Wall	1883-1905	931grt	15k	1883, Robert Duncan & Company, Port Glasgow
Irene	1885-1906	972grt	15k	1885, Harland & Wolff, Belfast
Olga	1887-1908	963grt	15k	1887, Laird Brothers, Birkenhead
Anglesey	1888-1911	963grt	15k	1888, Harland & Wolff, Belfast
Cambria	1889-1894	357grt	13k	1889, Laird Brothers, Birkenhead

Rosstrevor	1895-1926	1,065grt	16k	1895, Wm Denny & Brothers, Dumbarton
Connemara	1913-1916	1,106grt	18 ½k	1897, Wm Denny & Brothers, Dumbarton
Cambria / Arvonia	1897-1921	1,842grt	21k	1897, Wm Denny & Brothers, Dumbarton
Hibernia	1900-1914	1,862grt	21k	1900, Wm Denny & Brothers, Dumbarton
Anglia	1900-1914	1,862grt	21k	1900, Wm Denny & Brothers, Dumbarton
Scotia / Menavia	1902-1921	1,872grt	21k	1902, Wm Denny & Brothers, Dumbarton
Galtee More	1898-1926	1,112grt	17 ½k	1898, Wm Denny & Brothers, Dumbarton
South Stack	1900-1931	977grt	17 ½k	1900, Laird Brothers, Birkenhead
Snowden	1902-1936	1,021grt	17 ½k	1902, Laird Brothers, Birkenhead
Pick Me Up (Dredger)	1902-1968	170grt	8k	1902, Fleming & Ferguson Limited, Paisley
Elevator No. 1 (Coaling Elavator)	1903-?			1903, Dublin Dockyard
Slievemore	1904-1932	1,053grt	17 ½k	1904, Harland & Wolff, Belfast
Slieve Bawn	1905-1935	1,061grt	17 ½k	1905, Harland & Wolff, Belfast
Slieve Bloom	1908-1918	1,166grt	17 ½k	1907, Vickers, Sons & Maxim Limited, Barrow
Slieve Gallion	1908-1937	1,166grt	17 ½k	1908, Vickers, Sons & Maxim Limited, Barrow

Rathmore	1908-1927	1,569grt	20k	1908, Vickers, Sons & Maxim Limited, Barrow
Herald (Coaling Barge)	1910-?	347grt	5k	1910, Vickers, Sons & Maxim Limited, Barrow
Greenore	1912-1926	1,488grt	20 ½k	1912, Cammell Laird & Company, Birkenhead
Curraghmore / Duke of Abercorn	1919-1930	1,587grt	20 ½k	1919, Wm Denny & Brothers, Dumbarton
Anglia	1920-1924	3,460grt	24k	1920, Wm Denny & Brothers, Dumbarton
Hibernia / Hibernia II	1920-1949	3,458grt	24k	1920, Wm Denny & Brothers, Dumbarton
Cambria / Cambria II	1920-1949	3,445grt	24k	1920, Wm Denny & Brothers, Dumbarton
Scotia	1920-1940	3,441grt	24k	1920, Wm. Denny & Brothers, Dumbarton
Slieve Donard	1922-1954	1,116grt	16k	1922, Vickers Limited, Barrow in Furness
Mellifont	1928-1931	1,200grt	16 ½k	1903, Vickers Limited, Barrow in Furness
Colleen Bawn	1928-1931	1,200grt	16 ½k	1903, Vickers Limited, Barrow in Furness
Slieve Bloom	1930-1965	1,113grt	16k	1930, Wm Denny & Brothers, Dumbarton
Slieve More	1932-1965	1,397grt	17k	1932, Wm Denny & Brothers, Dumbarton
Slieve League	1935-1967	1,342grt	17k	1935, Wm Denny & Brothers, Dumbarton

Slieve Bawn	1937-1953 / 1965-	1,454grt	17k	1937, Wm Denny & Brothers, Dumbarton
Princess Maud	1946-1965	2,917grt	20k	1934, Wm Denny & Brothers, Dumbarton
Hibernia	1949-1976	4,973grt	21k	1949, Harland & Wolff, Belfast
Cambria	1949-1975	4,972grt	21k	1949, Harland & Wolff, Belfast
Slieve Donard	1960-1975	1,598grt	13 ½k	1960, Ailsa Shipbuilding Company, Troon
Holyhead Ferry 1 / Earl Leofric	1965-1975/78	3,879grt	20 ½k	1965, Hawthorn Leslie Limited, Newcastle
Harrogate	1965	871grt	13 ½k	1959, J. Lamont & Co. Ltd
Duke of Rothesay	1965/1975	5,075grt	21k	1956, Wm Denny & Brothers, Dumbarton
Caledonian Princess	1968 / 1976-1977	3,629grt	20 ½k	1961, Wm Denny & Brothers, Dumbarton
Dover / Earl Siward	1969 / 1973-1976 / 81	3,601grt	20 ½k	1965, Swan Hunter & Wigham Richardson
Darlington	1968	962grt	13 ½k	1958, J. Lamont & Co. Ltd, Clydebank
Selby	1969	962grt	13 ½k	1958, J. Lamont & Co. Ltd, Clydebank
Brian Boroime	1970-1989	4,098grt	14k	1970, Verolme Cork Dockyard, Cobh
Rhodri Mawr	1970-1989	4,098grt	14k	1970, Verolme Cork Dockyard, Cobh
Isle of Ely	1969-1972	866grt	15 ½k	1958, Goole Shipbuilding & Repairing, Goole
Colchester	1972	1,946grt	15 ½k	1959, Goole Shipbuilding & Repairing, Goole
Lord Warden	1971	3,333grt	20k	1952, Wm Denny & Brothers, Dumbarton

Duke of Argyll	1975	4,450grt	21k	1956, Harland & Wolff, Belfast
Duke of Lancaster	1975-1979	4,450grt	21k	1956, Harland & Wolff, Belfast
Avalon	1976-1980	6,584grt	21k	1963, Alexander Stephen & Sons, Linthouse, Glasgow
St Columba / Stena Hibernia / Stena Adventurer	1977-1996	7,836grt	20k	1977, Aalborg Værft, A/S, Aalborg, Denmark
Dalriada	1978	1,600grt	17 ½k	1971, Bröderne Lothes Skibsværft A/S, Haugesund, Norway
Stena Timer	1979	2,905grt	17k	1977, Österreichische Sciffswerften AG, Korneuburg, Austria
St Christopher / Stena Antrim	1981/1995	7,399grt	19k	1981, Harland & Wolff, Belfast
Prinsessan Desirée	1981	5,694grt	18k	Aalborg Værft, A/S, Aalborg, Denmark
St David	1981-1985/86	7,196grt	19k	1981, Harland & Wolff, Belfast
Stena Sailer / St Cybi	1987-1991	2,495grt	17k	1975, Verolme Cork Dockyard, Cobh
Seafreight Highway	1988	5,088grt	18k	1981, Appriania Marina di Carpara, Italy
Horsa / Stena Horsa	1990-1991	5,495grt	19 ½k	1972, Direction des Construction et Armes Navales, Brest
Stena Cambria	1991-1998	7,405grt	19 ½k	1980, Harland & Wolff, Belfast
Stena Galloway	1992	6,630grt	19k	1979, Harland & Wolff, Belfast
Stena Sea Lynx / Stena Lynx	1993-1994/1996-1997	3,331gt	38k	1993, Incat, Tasmania, Australia
Stena Sea Lynx II	1994	3,898gt	36k	1994, Incat, Tasmania, Australia
Stena Traveller	1995-1996	18,332gt	18k	1992, Fosen Mekaniske Verksteder, Norway

Stena Explorer	1996-	19,638gt	40k	1996, Finnyards, Rauma, Finland
Stena Challenger	1996-2001	18,523gt	19.5k	1990, Fosen Mek Verkteder, Norway
Stena Forwarder	2001-2003	24,000gt	22.5k	2001, Visentini, Trasporti, Italy
Stena Adventurer	2003-	43,532gt	22.5k	2003, Hyundai Heavy Industries, Ulsan, South Korea
Stena Seatrader	2006-2008	17,991gt	18.5k	1973, A/S Nakskov Skibsværft, Nakskov, Denmark
St David (Harbour Tug)	2006-	100dwt	11.5k	2006, Damen
Stena Nordica	2008-	24,206grt	25k	2001, Mitsubishi Heavy Industries, Shimonoseki, Japan
Stena Lynx III	2000- 2001/2010-2011	4,113grt	35k	1996, Incat, Tasmania, Australia

The *Stena Sea Lynx*. (Gary Davies / Maritime Photographic)

1994 'Sea Lynx' brochures – The Faster Option.

The *Stena Cambria* passes the *Isle of Inishmore* on the Admiralty Pier at Holyhead. (Dick Richards)

The *Stena Hibernia* passes the *Isle of Inishmore* at Holyhead. (Dick Richards)

Irish Ferries' *Saint Killian II*
briefly appeared at Holyhead.
(Brian Cleare)

The *Stena Hibernia* at Dun
Laoghaire Harbour mouth.
(Justin Merrigan)

The *Stena Hibernia* arriving
at the Inner Harbour berth at
Holyhead. (Justin Merrigan)

The original *Isle of Innisfree* at Holyhead on lifeboat day. (Ian Collard)

The purpose-built *Isle of Innisfree* on the calm waters of Dublin Bay. (Justin Merrigan)

Above left: Captain Richard Jones on the *Stena Hibernia*. (Justin Merrigan)

Above right: Captain Hugh Farrell on the *Stena Sea Lynx*. (Justin Merrigan)

Below: The *Stena Londoner* was a visitor to the Dun Laoghaire service in April 1996, becoming the last British ferry to carry the Sealink brand on the Irish Sea. (Justin Merrigan)

The *Stena Adventurer* at Dun Laoghaire in May 1996. (Justin Merrigan)

The *Stena Adventurer* and *Stena Lynx*. (Justin Merrigan)

The *Stena Traveller* at Holyhead. (Ian Collard)

The HSS *Stena Explorer* approaches Holyhead. (Gary Davies / Maritime Photographic)

The HSS *Stena Explorer* sails from Dun Laoghaire. (Ian Collard)

An aerial view of Dun Laoghaire Ferry Terminal, August 2006. (Peter Barrow)

Dun Laoghaire Harbour.
(Peter Barrow)

The *Express Aphrodite* at
Belfast on 5 May 1997.
(Alan Geddes)

Handover of the *Stena
Adventurer* by Holyhead's
Captain Peter Lockyer to
the ship's new Greek Master,
Belfast May, 1997. (Justin
Merrigan)

The *Stena
Challenger*
outward
from Dublin
Port. (Justin
Merrigan)

The *Stena
Cambria*
on the final
day of
conventional
service at Dun
Laoghaire,
3 May 1997.
(Justin
Merrigan)

Irish Ferries'
*Isle of
Inishmore.*
(Gary Davies /
Maritime
Photographic)

The *Stena Forwarder* on passage in a wild Irish Sea. (Derry Walsh)

The *Stena Europe* on relief duty at Holyhead under the command of Captain David Farrell. (John Lewis)

The *Stena Adventurer* as built in 2003. (Gary Davies / Maritime Photographic)

A busy day in Holyhead Harbour in 1985.

The *Stena Hibernia* passes *Stena Cambria* outside Holyhead Harbour in 1993. (Justin Merrigan Collection)

The HSS *Stena Explorer* pulls away from her berth at Holyhead in 1997.

The *Ulysses, Stena Adventurer* and *Jonathan Swift* at Holyhead, 2007.

Competitors at Dublin; Irish Ferries' *Ulysses* and Stena Line's *Stena Adventurer*. (Gary Davies / Maritime Photographic)

The *Stena Seatrader* following an extensive overhaul at Cammell Laird, Birkenhead. (Ian Collard)

The *Stena Nordica* in Dublin Bay on passage to Dublin. (Gordon Hislip)

The HSS *Discovery* (ex-*Stena Discovery*) bound for South America and the *Stena Explorer* on 1 October 2009. (Ronnie Roberts)

The tug *St David* working in Holyhead Harbour with the *Henty Pioneer* on 26 June 2010. (Ronnie Roberts)

The Holyhead harbour tug *St David* at speed outside Holyhead Harbour. (Captain Wyn Parry)

The Holland America cruise liner *Westerdam* at Holyhead on 7 August 2010. (Captain Wyn Parry)

The *Duke of Lancaster* languishes at Llanerch-y-Mor, North Wales, in 2010. (Ronnie Roberts)

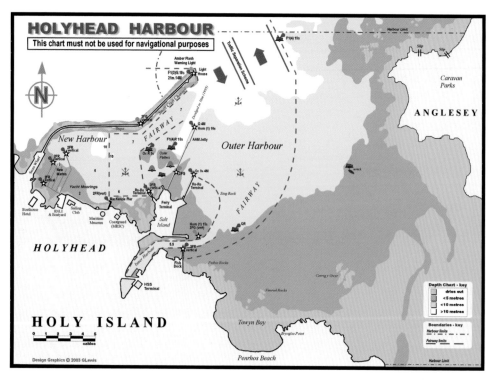

Map of Holyhead Harbour. (Courtesy of Stena Line)

The *Stena Adventurer*. (Gary Davies / Maritime Photographic)

The *Stena Adventurer.* (Derry Walsh)

The *Stena Lynx III* in Dublin Bay. (Gordon Hislip)

The *Stena Lynx III* sails past HSS *Stena Explorer* at Holyhead. (Ronnie Roberts)

The *Jonathan Swift* arriving at Holyhead. (Gary Davies / Maritime Photographic)

ACKNOWLEDGEMENTS

The authors wish to thank the following for their kind contribution: Captain Wyn Parry, Shipping and Port Manager, Stena Line, Holyhead; Captain Glynne Pritchard; Captain John Bakewell; David Jones; Kenneth Whyte; Ronald Roberts; John Hodgkinson; Gary Davies, Maritime Photographic; Captain Simon Coate, Harbour Master, Dun Laoghaire; Chris Howell, Dave Smith – Pictureships, Derry Walsh, Gordon Hislip and Ian Scott Taylor.

A special word of thanks to Mary Gallagher for access to the Brinsley Sheridan Collection.

AUTHORS

Justin Merrigan

Justin grew up in Ireland, within the sight and sounds of Dun Laoghaire Harbour where the activities surrounding the Holyhead Irish Sea ferries soon became a fascination. The harbour was his playground and as well as his rescue boat activities for Dublin Bay's yacht racing, he also served as a crew member and committee member of the Dun Laoghaire branch of the Royal National Lifeboat Institution.

Initially joining Stena Sealink Line, he later served, as agent, as Terminal Manager for Sea Containers' Dublin Port operations before joining Australian fast ferry pioneer Incat as PR Officer in 2000. Residing in Hobart, he soon acquainted himself with the local scene and is an associate member of the Master Mariners Association of Tasmania.

Justin has travelled extensively across the ferry world and, in 2009, joined Brisbane-based builder Aluminium Boats Australia as Marketing & International Sales Manager.

Ian Collard

Ian was born and bred only half a mile from Birkenhead Docks, which as a child he used as his playground. He was given a camera for his tenth birthday and was taken on a day trip to the Isle of Man the following year by his mother. This was the start of an interest in ships and photography that has given him so much enjoyment over the years.

Obtaining a Mersey Docks & Harbour Company photography pass, he spent most of his weekends photographing the maritime scene in Liverpool and Birkenhead Docks and on the River Mersey. This was at the time when containerisation was developing and many of the old conventional cargo vessels were in the process of being replaced by larger ships. Ian also developed an interest in coastal freight and passenger ships and obtained a summer Isle of Man Steam Packet 'sailing contract' on his sixteenth birthday, enabling him to sail regularly on that company's vessels. He was also able to witness and photograph the development of the car ferry on the various routes in the Irish Sea and to travel on several maiden voyages on these vessels.

Since taking early retirement as a social work manger he has written several books on ships and maritime-related industries such as the Mersey Docks & Harbour Company and the history of Cammell Laird and its ships. He still sails when he can and is never happier than standing on the deck of a ship in the middle of the Irish Sea in a roaring gale.